THE ZAKRO MASTER
AND HIS PLACE
IN PREHISTORY

by

JUDITH WEINGARTEN

Paul Åströms förlag
Göteborg 1983

737,4
W4332

AE G-0812

TO

MY MOTHER AND STEPFATHER

CONTENTS

The Zakro sealings are a unique source of evidence for
the art and administration of a provincial palace town on the
eve of its violent destruction. It is unique artistic evidence
in that, unlike the contemporary sealing hoards from Ayia
Triada and Chania, many seals seem to have been the work of
a single artist, he who may fairly be called "the Zakro Master."
Perhaps as many as seventy works from his hand remain, an
oeuvre unrivalled in prehistory. The sealings equally provide
unique insight into local administrative practices, based, as
they largely are, on an elaborate system of stamping and
counterstamping which hardly exists elsewhere. This study
examines the sealings from both viewpoints, that of art as
well as of administration.

Part I examines the implications of the stamping system,
the complicated patterns of seal usage revealed on the clay
nodules. What can it tell us about the seal owners and their
relationships, or of the bureaucracy of the town?

When D.G. Hogarth excavated the sealings at Zakro in 1901,
pottery classifications were still being worked out. His
"painted Mycenaean ware" can now be better placed in its true
chronological position. In Chapter I, we review the pottery
associated with the sealings and describe their discovery.
Using a purely analytic and statistical approach, we then
examine the sealing system (Chapter II). We discover two
strands in the system, one fairly straightforward, but the
other needing quite a bit of unravelling. Hogarth thought
that the sealing combinations reflected the use of two or
three sided seals rather than a system of counterstamping.
This opinion invites us to consider the size, shape, and style
of each impression in its combination(s) to determine if a
multifaceted seal could have been responsible. Exploring
the combinations makes the interplay of the seals somewhat
clearer. We next turn to the clay nodules themselves, their
shapes and types, and consider what this once tractable
material tells us about the sealing system (Chapter III). Then,
a fascinating question:- what did the sealings actually seal?
(Chapter IV). Unusually clear traces of the sealing imprints
are left on the fire-baked nodules; these show exactly where

the clay touched the object sealed. After examining a fair
number of such nodule "bottoms", we can propose a solution to
at least part of the problem.

Part II turns to art, and the work of the Zakro Master.
His unusual visions have excited comment since their discovery:-
what, if anything, can they mean? Appreciation of his work
varies enormously:- is it excellent, of fine technique, or
crude, even incompetent. Or, are such questions irrelevant
and the artist merely mad? The review of such opinions (Chapter
ii/I) reminds us (oddly) of the reception of modernism in art.

Some of the problems raised in Chapter ii/I are caused by
a lurking uncertainty as to which exact works are by his hand,
and which are not. Chapter ii/II establishes, it is to be hoped,
objective criteria for recognizing his work so that we may view
his surviving oeuvre as a whole.

Every artist, mad or sane, is a child of his time. He
has roots, training, a tradition. Chapter ii/III tries to
identify this tradition, to place the Zakro Master within an
art-historical context. Possibly, his surviving works represent
more than one period in his life.Can we follow any lines of
development, any artistic evolution? Even 3,500 years after
the event, the urge to understand something of his interests
and preoccupations as an artist is irresistible; is it also
worthwhile? (Chapter ii/IV).

The Zakro Master probably did live and work at Zakro, a
town in touch with the Near East and, possibly, trading direct
with Egypt. Foreign artistic traditions probably were visible
at Zakro; was the Zakro Master receptive? We identify two
areas where foreign influence might have entered his work,
never as direct copies but in invigorating adaptations
(Chapter ii/V). A strongly original artist may manipulate his
heritage and something of his innovations may enter contemporary
traditions. In turn, he thus can be seen to influence other
artists. Even at this distance, we can at least try to discover
the Zakro Master's influence on others (Chapter ii/VI).

Given the gaps in our records, the effort to appreciate
and criticize a prehistoric artist is, necessarily, only a
first step. We hope, however, that we shall emerge with a
slightly better understanding of his work, local traditions,
and, perhaps, his place in prehistory.

The Zakro Master and His Place in Prehistory is based
on my M. Litt. thesis, submitted at Oxford in October 1981,
but revised to incorporate much new material studied during
two further sessions at the Heraklion Museum.[1] The Zakro
combinations and their frequency of appearance may now be
taken as definitive for all practical purposes.

In addition to the natural satisfaction at the publication of this work, there is the added pleasure of being able
to thank those who have helped and contributed during the
course of my researches. First, I must thank my supervisor,
Professor John Boardman, who proposed the study of the Zakro
sealings as a marriage of my interests in art and archaeology.
I am extremely grateful to him for his encouragement of the
unorthodox in my approach. I am also enormously indebted to
Mervyn Popham who bore with me through all the demands of the
administrative chapters and who greatly helped bring order to
the turmoil of Zakro numbers. I am grateful to many at the
Ashmolean Museum, particularly to Michael Vickers, Assistant
Keeper, for his always generous interpretation of access to
the collection . I would also warmly thank Professor Dr Y.
Sakellarakis, Director of the Heraklion Museum, and Dr G.
Tzedakis, Ephor at Chania, for the privilege of studying
collections in their care. I gratefully acknowledge a grant
from the Craven Fund which allowed me to visit Greece when
most necessary. Finally, I join the long list of glyptic
scholars who are much indebted to Dr Ingo Pini of the CMS
Redaktion at Marburg for the opportunity to study his superb
photographs and for the benefit of his advice, always
generously given.

In the Heraklion Museum, I had the opportunity to take
plasticine impressions of many of the better-baked nodules
from Zakro and a handful from Ayia Triada. These, of course,
reproduce the original gems (the true positives) rather than
the seal impressions. To return to the desired negatives, I
made silicone rubber casts (Rhodorsil RTV 1150A + catalyst
58R) of the plasticine. The casts, photographed at the
Institute of Archaeology, Oxford, lose something of the
sharpness of line of the originals but compensate for this
deficiency by the clarity of detail. Additional photographs
were kindly supplied by Dr Ingo Pini (Nr 44, 76, 86 170) and

Dr Carl Albiker (Nr 43 and 87). The remaining photographs
are taken from negatives used in the original publication by
D.G. Hogarth (<u>JHS</u> xxii Pl. vi - x).[2] I am most grateful to
the Society for the Promotion of Hellenic Studies for trans-
ferring them from the early glass negatives to film (Pl. ix
was missing, never having returned from the printer in 1902)
and their allowing me to make use of them in this study.

1. A slightly revised Chapter IV has been published in
    <u>Kadmos</u> 22 (1983): 8 - 13.
2. Sealing numbers up to and including Nr 144 refer to
    the original Hogarth numbers in Hogarth 1902b; numbers
    Nr 146 (there is no Nr 145) - Nr 200 refer to Levi
    1929b; more recently discovered seal-types are
    numbered sequentially, Nr 201 etc.

PART I: THE ZAKRO SEALINGS

CHAPTER I

DISCOVERY OF THE SEALINGS

> I resti dell'antica città sono considervoli
> non tanto per la quantità ed estensione, quanto
> per la mole delle mura e dei blocchi, i più
> grossi che io mi abbia visto in Creta.
>
> Professor L. Mariani, 1895.[1]

The sealings were found in House A, most conspicuous of a
group of buildings excavated by D.G. Hogarth on the eastern,
lower spur at Zakro in 1901 (Pl. 2A). Built of true Cyclopean
masonry on the highest point of the spur, the house opens to
the southwest and dominates the shallow cultivated ravine
below. The Palace, almost due south, would not have been
visible from House A, though roof-to-roof contact cannot be
entirely ruled out. Only eight rooms of House A survived in
plan though Hogarth considered this but the forepart of a
larger complex built on the crown of the spur.[2]

The entrance hall in House A -- one of the very first
"Mycenaean" houses excavated on Crete -- presented a remarkable sight (Pl. 1A). Just inside the doorway were three
basins built into the tarazza floor, two joined by a paved
channel.[3] But the first object to have struck the eye of a
visitor would have been a square pillar, its stone base
covered with blue-painted plaster, above which rose a wooden
column, the burnt remains of which were found in situ. Though
this pillar stood centrally in the entrance hall, it seemed
of little, if any, structural use for it stood barely 20 cm.
from a massive brick wall which itself measured between 80 -
140 cm. in thickness. A doorway led from this chamber into a
collapsed stairway which must once have led to an upper floor.
In the "rubbish" of this collapse were found substantial
fragments of two virtually identical rhyta in the finest
Marine Style.[4]

Another broad doorway led north from the entrance hall
into two large rooms. The farther room, viii , contained five
large pithoi, nine amphorae, and 13 conical cups placed upside
down. Room vii had been decorated with painted plaster, bits
of which were recovered showing traces of a yellow pattern
on blue ground. The room was paved with burnt brick tiles
laid on pack earth, above which

2

at a height of /¯45 cm._/ from the floor, and under
a mass of disordered bricks ... occurred a remarkable
group of objects, lying at all angles as if fallen from
above. The first to appear were fragments of a large
bronze knife or sword; then two almost perfect painted
vases of the "hole-mouth" strainer form with parts of
about ten other painted vases all belonging to the
Mycenaean type (fig. 43); then two heavy bronze tools
... and four massive round bronze points ... (fig. 44)
.... Finally there were scattered over a small and
roughly circular space among and about the bronzes an
immense number (nearly 500) of well preserved clay
nodules bearing impressions of intaglios. Most of these
have two or three faces, and were evidently seals
attached to documents. Among them lay a broken baked
clay wedge ... showing obliterated characters in the
/¯Linear A_/ script on both faces. and a roughly
circular tablet ... in the same script.

The sealings all have been hardened by fire but
whether in the baking or accidentally by the conflagration which evidently destroyed the structure in which I
found them, it is impossible to say. The fact that they
were found over a restricted and roughly circular area
suggests that they had fallen all together from a height
on the collapse of some receptable in which they had
been stored. (Hogarth 1901: 132-33).

The nodules were thus found in a closed, though not sealed,
destruction deposit along with abundant pottery. The pottery
illustrated in "fig. 43", which ought to have been that found
with the sealings, was merely captioned "Typical Painted Vases
from House A", and, indeed, except for one "strainer" does not
seem to fit Hogarth's description (Pl. 2B). More pottery was
published by Dawkins but only a few of the illustrated vases
were from House A (Pl. 3C) and, as was the practice at the
time, no sherds were shown.[5] Still, the pottery is clearly
LMIA in type, a classification accepted by Evans and Pendlebury.[6] Furumark first proposed, however, -- and Platon's
recent excavations at Zakro confirm -- that LMIA-style pottery
was still being made on East Cretan sites at a time when LMIB-
style vases, such as Marine Style and advanced floral styles,
were being produced, probably at Knossos, and exported to
provincial towns.[7] This is his "Sub-LMIA" period. This must
be the period of House A's destruction for the combination of
conservative LMIA-type pottery and two Marine Style rhyta
seems irrefutable.[8]

3

Furthermore, the style of the Marine Style rhyta is remarkably similar to that of another Marine Style rhyton found in the destruction deposit of the Treasury of the Central Shrine in the Palace itself (Pl. 3A-B). Betancourt, in his study of Marine Style, considers the three rhyta to be by the same hand.[9] Thus, the destruction dates of House A and the Palace, an undisputed LMIB destruction, cannot be separated by much, if any, time. This suggests that there may have been two contemporary administrative centres at Zakro:- one in our House A on the northeast hill -- an area described by Platon as Palace annexes[10] -- and a centre, as expected,within the Palace buildings.[11] The palatial centre is in the West Wing where, in a room dubbed "The Archive", were found 14 more or less complete Linear A tablets. The deep russet colour of the fill in the Archive showed, however, how much had been lost:- many more tablets must have disintegrated before the final fire could bake them hard. Only four sealings were found with the tablets, though, of course, many more could have disappeared in the shapeless mass of crushed tablets.[12] The Archive was connected with the Central Shrine which, in fact, opened into it on both sides.

In House A, we recall, the entrance hall had been furnished with a structurally redundant square pillar. Hogarth rather inclined to view it as a pillar shrine although its open aspect seems to tell against this interpretation.[13] The two rhyta, paralleling the more numerous rhyta of the Palace's Central Shrine, might have had a religious purpose. Similarly, near the palatial shrine, an entire bronze "tool-kit" -- saws, hammers, chisels, knives, etc. -- had tumbled from above into the lustral basin, reminding us of the more modest fall of bronze knives, mattocks and drills (Pl. 2C) into Room vii of House A where they lay with the sealings. The analogy should not be pushed too far but there is a possibility that House A did contain a modest replica of the main administrative cum religious services. Why this should be so and why any administration should be needed on the northeast hill, far from the harbour and, it now seems likely, at the very inland edge of the town,[14] are questions which might better be answered after a study of the sealings.

4

1. Mariani (<u>MonAnt</u> vi 294-95) also thought that he had found a temple at Zakro, probably Hogarth's House A.

2. Excavations by Platon have now reached the edges of House A (Pl. 1B) and it seems that Hogarth's surmise is correct. Platon may uncover a building three times the size of that revealed by Hogarth (personal communication).

3. Hogarth 1901: 144 suggested that a second plaster channel led to a shallow tank in the south part of the room and that the whole arrangement was, perhaps, a kind of wine press.

4. Hogarth 1902a: Pl- xii,1 (our Pl. 3A). Two large fragments, the almost complete neck and lip and a part of the upper body, of the second rhyton are now Ashmolean Museum 785/86.

5. Dawkins 1903.

6. <u>PM</u> i 701; Pendlebury 1939: 201.

7. Furumark 1950: 154. Inexplicably, in 1972: 80, Furumark removed the Marine Style rhyta from House A and assigns them to the "unstratified dumps". This directly contradicts the excavator's explicit testimony (Hogarth 1901: 132 and, again, 1902a: 333 "...precise findspot was the doorway between room 3 and 5 ....").

8. Irrefutable or not, Platon (Platon and Brice 1975:39) continues to argue that House A is a LMIA destruction. However, he ignores the evidence of the Marine Style rhyta and has published no new pottery from the area to support his contention. Perhaps more recent excavations will yield new evidence. Compare Palaikastro IV in Dawkins 1905: 274-75. On the reluctance of Zakro potters to abandon old techniques, see Popham 1967: 339.

9. Betancourt 1973: 333 (his Group D). Mountjoy 1977: 559 - 60, however, denies that they are all three by the same hand, though she does not doubt their close similarities.

10. Platon 1971b: 226-32 discusses the many buildings he has excavated on the northeast hill but does not explain in detail why he considers them to be Palace annexes. Presumably, this is based on the fact that the Palace lies much lower than these buildings and no prince wishes to

be looked down upon by outsiders. One could go further and declare simply that no prince likes to be looked down upon. This is but one of the many peculiarities of the Palace at Zakro.

11. Two separate administrative centres coexisted at Ayia Triada as well. There, the major archive was in the town while a few tablets were found with the mass of sealings in the Palace.

12. I would like to thank Professor N. Platon for allowing me to examine these new sealings which remain, for the moment, unpublished.

13. Hogarth 1902: 120; Nilsson 1950: 242 considers that it is indeed a pillar room. Since we do not know anything of the upper storey, one must maintain some reservations about its lack of structural purpose. Still, as Nilsson _ibid_ Chapter vii indirectly points out, structural function is not incompatible with sacred character. It may be worth mentioning that, at Knossos, two small connecting Pillar Crypts in the West Wing of the Palace are associated with several rooms where sealings were found (see Gill 1965: fig. 1), not least, above and to the east of the East Pillar Crypt, the Tripartite Columnar Shrine with its numerous "Mother-of-the-Mountain" sealings (PM ii 796 - 810).

14. Before House A on the southwest is a roughly paved road, in front of which lies a terrace, about five meters wide, after which the ground falls away steeply into the ravine. Although there are scattered houses on the hill to the northeast, House A is farthest away from the sea, over 300 meters from the nearest point. Since most of that distance is uphill, House A cannot be considered conveniently situated for any harbour business.

CHAPTER II

THE MULTIPLE SEALING SYSTEM

One of the most remarkable things about the Zakro sealings, and that which sets them apart from sealings found elsewhere on the island, is that most of the nodules are stamped with seal impressions on two or three faces. Of the 525 more or less intact nodules which I have studied, 120 are stamped on three sides, 240 on two sides and 165 on just a single side; there are thus 1005 seal impressions made by the often repeated use of approximately 214 seal-types.[1] It is this peculiarity, which has received surprisingly little comment in the 80 years since discovery, that this chapter examines in the hope that so pronounced a local habit might shed some light on local administrative practice.

If each seal-type represents an individual, some 214 individuals had some connection with the affairs of House A.[2] It would be tidy to assume that they all shared much the same connections with these affairs -- whatever they may have been -- but the pattern of stamping and, perhaps, counterstamping, suggests some system of discrimination. When one separates the nodules into the two most obvious groups -- those that are single-stamped from those that are stamped twice or thrice -- it becomes clear that we are dealing with two quite different systems and, possibly, two different functions. For simplicity, I shall call the first group the Single-Sealing System (SSS) and the second the Multiple-Sealing System (MSS).

First, the most notable fact:- there is virtually no overlap between the seal-types appearing in the SSS and those appearing in the MSS. Thus, with but one exception,[3] the 93 seal-types of the SSS never appear in the MSS and, equally, the 121 of the MSS are never individually used in the SSS. Pure chance cannot possibly account for this level of apartheid.

Similarly, chance alone cannot be responsible for the significant differences in the iconography displayed in each of the systems. Detailed analysis of SSS and MSS iconography is given in Table 1.[4] The SSS shows a strong preference for naturalistic seal-types (65.6% of the total) whereas these make up a much smaller proportion of MSS seal-types (21.5%). On the other hand, the fantastic types which account for Zakro's peculiar flavour are concentrated in the MSS:-

eliminating pan-Cretan monsters (i.e. griffins to Minoan Genius in Table 1) leaves fully 65% of the MSS dedicated to what may fairly be called local monsters; such monsters account for only 5.4% of the SSS. Put another way, nearly 95% of the SSS would be equally at home anywhere on Crete (cf.: Ayia Triada and Chania in Table 1) while only 33% of the MSS seal-types would fail to raise eyebrows were they found elsewhere. Yet one cannot label the SSS as foreign in any meaningful sense.[5] Eight of the 61 MSS combinations lack even a single local monster while another 15 combinations mix naturalistic and fantasy types (Table 2 and 3). Still, the naturalistic and the fantasy do not bond easily:- such combinations are usually found just once or, but rarely, twice.[6]

Another factor to be considered is frequency of seal use and, here, the SSS is noticeably weaker:- 70, in fact, only appear once in the records while the whole SSS only accounts for 165 out of more than one thousand impressions. One may say that the intensity of seal usage is significantly less in the SSS than in the MSS:-

	SSS		MSS	
	n.	%	n.	%
Ten or more uses	2	2.1	12	19.4
Between 2 - 9 uses	21	22.6	24	38.7
One use only	70	75.3	26	41.9
	93	100%	62	100.%

Seal usage is more intensive in the MSS and it is also more evenly spread:- nearly 60% of the combinations in the MSS appear more than once in the records against just one-quarter of SSS seal-types.

Finally, in those cases where we can reasonably recreate the shape of the impressing agent from a study of impression outlines, we find yet another difference between the SSS and the MSS:- the MSS is made up almost totally of lentoids while the SSS preserves a more varied collection:-

	SSS	MSS
Signets	9	5
Lentoids	44(63%)	87(88%)
Elliptical/glandular	11	5
Flattened cylinder	5	2
Rectangular prism	1	-

8

We can now say with some confidence that the SSS and the
MSS represent two systems which may or may not have run in
tandem at Zakro. Certainly, they have much in common, not
least that they were found together within a very restricted
area.[7] Yet sharp differences may be said to distinguish the
systems and one may be justified in postulating that they
served some different purpose. It is therefore time to study
the MSS in more detail and examine its almost unique system of
stamping and counterstamping.

The MSS is divided into two parts:- 40 pairs (nodules
stamped twice) and 22 triplets (nodules stamped thrice). It
is further divided into:-

Invariable Combinations (Table 2)
However many times a seal-type appears, it only appears in
the same fixed combination with one or two other types and
this combination, pair or triplet, never varies.[8]

Variable Combinations (Table 3)
A seal-type appears in more than one combination. It may
appear only in pairs, only in triplets, or may "overlap",
appearing in both pairs and triplets.

At the risk of anticipating a conclusion, it may be stated
that, generally, but not always, pairs appear on nodules with
two faces and triplets on nodules with three faces and that
this is the only apparent difference between them.[9] We therefore feel justified in treating them together as part of the
same overall system.

I. INVARIABLE COMBINATIONS

The Invariable Combinations (Table 2) are made up of 25
pairs and 8 triplets using a total of 74 individual seal-
types. Hogarth probably had these combinations in mind when
he wrote:-

it is at least highly probable that the twice and
thrice stamped nodules were impressed each by a single two
or three faced seal as are commonly found in East Crete....
(Hogarth 1902b: 90)

The "three faced seal" can only be a three-sided prism, a
shape indeed long favoured in East Crete, at least in the
Early and Middle Bronze Age.[10] But the shape is no longer
popular in the Late Bronze Age and my survey of the literature
was only able to discover 56 probable LBA examples, few of
9

which are securely dated and only one of which is attributed to East Crete.[11] Thirty-five of the 56 prisms are of amygdaloid/ glandular shape and could not be responsible for the lentoid-like impressions of the MSS (see page 8 above). Twenty-one, however, have spherical or slightly elliptical faces which would make impressions indistinguishable from a lentoid; these seem restricted to the LBA.[12] Prisms of this shape are rarely engraved on all three faces:-

Engraved on three faces	5
Engraved on two faces	14
Engraved on one face	2
	21

Given their history, it is not surprising that most of the LBA examples adopt a talismanic or quasi-talismanic subject; only 16 of the 56 have a naturalistic style but these 16 include 15 of the spherical/elliptical types (Pl. 4, 5, 6).

Another possibility -- though whether Hogarth had it in mind is doubtful -- are lentoids engraved on both faces though these could not account, of course, for the triplets. A search of the literature brought to light 24 such examples, all but one of which may confidently be dated to MMIII or the Late Bronze Age (Table 5 ; Pl. 7,8).[13] Though it is quite wrong to generalize from such a tiny collection, it is perhaps significant that -- in contrast to the naturalistic prisms already examined -- many of the double-engraved lentoids have monster-type subjects:- 9a, 10b, 11b, 12a, 15a, 19b (super-imposed frontal human head), 21a, 21b, and 22a (though 12a and 22a are but pan-Cretan griffins). And it may be of interest that the only purported direct copy of local monsters of Zakro type occurs on a double-engraved seal (here made an honorary lentoid:- Table 5 , 2), a reel-shaped stone seal.[14]

Thus the theoretical possibility exists that some of the fixed combinations could be the result of using double-engraved lentoids. In the Invariable Combinations, we can rule out this possibility in twelve of the 33 combinations based on incompatibility of style, shape or size of the combined impressions. The remaining combinations (asterisked in Table 2) _might_ include two or even (in one case) three impressions made by a single stone; we shall return to this possibility in more detail after our examination of the MSS Combinations.

The first group (MSS Nr 1 - 8) contains purely naturalistic seal-types, very much a minority taste within the MSS. Equally nonconformist is the varity of impressing agents (as far as this can be reasonably recreated from impression outlines):- this small group boasts four (possibly five) signet rings, two (possibly three) ellipses, two flattened cylinders and only four lentoids ... against 88% probable lentoids in the MSS as a whole! MSS Nr 6, though unpretentious in subject and shape, is a noteworthy pair:- Doro Levi, who published the nodule, considered the seals related in a narrative sense, i.e. the hunter of Nr 190 attacks the lion of Nr 154.[15] If correct, this must mean either simultaneous engraving or a symbiotic relationship between two seal owners.

Both signet-signet combinations in this group are also remarkable. MSS Nr 1 -- the most frequent total combination in the MSS -- pairs a cult procession with a Taurokathapsia, undoubtedly an aristocratic combination. One tends, of course, to elevate proprietors of cult scenes but the very next pair brings us down with a bump:- a cult scene is joined by the hindquarters of a scratching dog. Cult and Tauro-kathapsia are again paired in the second signet-signet set (MSS Nr 5). The cult ring, a seated goddess receiving an offering, is a near duplicate of the scene on the famous "matrix" from Knossos, evidence, perhaps, of contemporaneous-ness but not necessarily travel of the ring's owner.[16] The comparable ring at Knossos was always stamped alone; its use in combination at Zakro underlines the strength of local habit.

The next group (MSS 9 - 12) combines naturalistic and fantasy subjects, all of which exist in just a single example, usually badly damaged.

The majority of the Invariable Combinations are purely fantasy seal-types or types considered "neutral" such as geometric designs and buildings (MSS 13 - 33). We shall only discuss a few of them in any detail, choosing those which may best display their underlying relationships.[17]

MSS Nr 13/Frequency: 33/Nr 71 + 89 _ The seal-types share quite strong formal links:- the outline of the butterfly wings of the sphinx may have suggested the wavy line border (unique in Minoan glyptic) of its partner; the rosettes

within its wings and its fantail share much the same formal
balance as the waz with its lotus above.

MSS Nr 14/Frequency: 19/Nr 57 + 73 - The connecting link is
the double-axe; these are the only two double-axes to appear
in any fantasy seal-types at Zakro. Even the strongly incurved
shape of the axe above the Lion Mask is repeated in the double-
axe design of its partner.

MSS Nr 15/Frequency: 16/Nr 36 + 64 - The running winged figure
and the Boar Mask seem utterly unrelated. Some relationship,
however, must exist since a minor variant of our Boar Mask
appears with another running winged figure in MSS Nr 21. This
type of "look-alike" replacement, more common in the Variable
Combinations, argues an underlying logic of pairing, lost to
us, but nonetheless real.

MSS Nr 17/Frequency: 15/Nr 23 + 52 - This combination suggests
thematic as well as formal connections. Both seals illustrate
a bird-head theme; even the shape of the heads is very close.
The Bird-Lady's upraised arms reflect the structure of the
protomes while her row of breasts follows the line of their
connecting element. Her fantail skirt, too, may be hinted at
by the thick fringe of strokes above the lotus.

MSS Nr 22/Frequency: 2/Nr 70 + 77 - The "palm trees" are badly
broken but one can easily match their outline and branch
stalks in the bat's wings adorning a most unusual a tergo view
of a sphinx.

MSS Nr 23/Frequency: 2/Nr 49 + 130 - The unusual lattice-work
in the towers' structure mirrors the lattice-work of the
helmet between the dog heads. More than chance may oppose a
building with helmet:- a gate shrine pairs with a Bird-Lady
wearing Plumed Helmet (MSS Nr 45/46); a helmet floats to the
left of the building on Nr 131 (MSS 47/48).

MSS Nr 28/Frequency: 19/Nr 44 + 48 + 78 - Really a pair plus
one (Nr 78 is a larger impression). Nr 44 + 48 strongly echo
each other:- the floral abstraction is formally the gorgon
upside down; even dots in the one's meander may have become
the other's "eyes". We cannot know if the gorgon draws in the
Cherub or if the Cherub is part of another pattern.

MSS Nr 29/Frequency: 7/Nr 25 + 45 + 53 - Again an imbalance in
size (Nr 25 is larger than the other two impressions) but one

which does not destroy the visual link of three fantails --
though those of Nr 45 and 53 are stylistically closer. Compare
this combination with that of MSS Nr 17:- the gorgon, upside
down, mimics the Bird-Lady with upraised arms; both join with
bird protomes.

MSS Nr 30/Frequency: 3/Nr 58 + 84 + 74 - The logic of this
triplet is not apparent but it is obvious that no two of the
impressions could have come from the same stone:- Nr 58 is
smaller than 74 while 84 is slightly elliptical in shape.

MSS Nr 31/Frequency:2/Nr 81 + 82 + 108 - The two bucrania are
variations on a single theme:- not only are they drawn in the
same manner but they share the trick of overlapping perspective, presumably to enhance the illusion of depth:- Nr 81 has
a bird passing behind the bucranium's horn while Nr 82 has his
horn twisting behind his head. Nr 108 is from a slightly
larger gem.

MSS Nr 33/Frequency: 1/Nr 38 + 167 + 68 - The two animal masks
suggest a natural pairing but neither size nor shape nor style
eliminates the Bird-Lady. This is the only triplet that hangs
together on all three counts.

II. VARIABLE COMBINATIONS

There are 29 Variable Combinations (Table 3) using 45
(legible) seal-types, which may conveniently be divided into
ten sets. We shall describe each set in turn.

MSS Nr 34/Frequency: 1/Nr 2 + 62
MSS Nr 35/Frequency: 1/Nr 2 + 26
MSS Nr 36/Frequency: 2/Nr 26 + 66

MSS Nr 35 can be considered the pivotal combination:- this
pair breaks up, each half to recombine with a Boar Mask.

MSS Nr 37/Frequency: 1/Nr 12/13 + 75
MSS Nr 38/Frequency: 1/Nr 12/13 + 87
MSS Nr 39/Frequency: 2/Nr 12/13 + 113
MSS Nr 40/Frequency: 2/Nr 12/13 + 184
MSS Nr 41/Frequency: 1/Nr 12/13 + 175

In each case the scene of human combat pairs with a local
fantasy type in an interesting series of alternations:- the
sphinx, Nr 75, is but a variation of the winged lion, Nr 184,
itself a stylistic variation of the winged humanoids, Nr 175.
13

The leonine types continue in the lion's head, Nr 113. The
intrusion of a bucranium, Nr 87, might signal a lion-bull
interchange /⁻cf.: MSS Nr 30 = Lion Mask + Bucranium + Sphinx;
note also the metamorphosis of the Bucranium with wings and
small animals, Nr 81, into Lion Masks similarly adorned, Nr 57
and 58⁷.

MSS Nr 42/Frequency: 1/Nr 15 + 37 + 54
MSS Nr 43/Frequency: 1/Nr 15 + 59 + 135
MSS Nr 44/Frequency: 1/Nr 15 + 218

No pattern is apparent in this very damaged, fragmentary set.

MSS Nr 45/Frequency: 5/Nr 24 + 112 + 60
MSS Nr 46/Frequency: 2/Nr 24 + 112 + 105

Guarding the gate shrine are two quasi-naturalistic lions in
heraldic pose (NB: the helmet on the Bird-Lady; see above,
page 12). Do the lions of Nr 112 draw in the Lion Mask, Nr
60, and, indeed, the galloping lions of the next combination,
Nr 105? If so, it suggests that a part, the mask, may have
the value of the whole. What is especially interesting in
this set is the vertical as well as horizontal Lion-Lion link.

MSS Nr 47/Frequency: 1/Nr 51 + 131 + 19
MSS Nr 48/Frequency: 1/Nr 51 + 131 + 85

Here, the lions and their building split, perhaps, into two
images (NB: the helmet floating to the left in Nr 131; see the
previous set). This Lion-Building pair attracts, not other
lions, but, first, a Minotaur, then -- the part indeed equal
to the whole? -- a bucranium. Since a Minotaur is no more
than a human body with a bull's head, is it an ancient wit who
paired it with this bucranium wearing, not horns, but human
legs?

MSS Nr 49/Frequency: 17/Nr 21 + 61 + 28
MSS Nr 50/Frequency: 4/Nr 21 + 61 + 29
MSS Nr 49A-50A/Frequency: 1/ Nr 21 + 61A + 28 or 29

Superficially a Bird-Lady/Boar Mask/Bird-Lady combination, the
set displays two subtle interchanges:- both the Boar Mask and
the second Bird-Lady has a "look-alike" (it is a pity that MSS
Nr 49A-50A is so damaged that we cannot tell if the third seal-
type is Nr 28 or 29 or, conceivably, yet another variant).
How, one wonders, did the local administration distinguish
these combinations, or was there, in fact, no need to do so?

MSS Nr 51/Frequency: 1/Nr 22 + 63
MSS Nr 52/Frequency: 1/Nr 22 + 56
MSS Nr 53/Frequency: 3/Nr 63 + 56
In the style of country dancing, each couple splits up and
takes another partner (a + b, b + c, a + c). On the surface,
each seal-type looks quite different yet stylistic links are
surprisingly close:- the Boar Mask's knobbed tusks follow the
shape of the main "Snake Frames" (is this the right way up?) as
do the Bird Protomes above the Lion Mask. Thus, the abstract
"Snake Frames" design may be composed of elements from each of
its partners, perhaps a whole made from their parts.

MSS Nr 54/Frequency: 4/Nr 69 + 67 + 30
MSS Nr 55/Frequency: 1/Nr 69 + 171 + ?
With two Lion Masks in the first combination, it is tempting
to "read" the utterly damaged seal-type as Nr 67, or a variant,
but this is unjustified.

MSS Nr 56/Frequency: 15/Nr 90 + 132 + 33
MSS Nr 57/Frequency: 3/Nr 90 + 132 + 173
MSS Nr 58/Frequency: 30/Nr 90 + 132 + 88
The most common pair in our records, Nr 90 + 132 (48 times),
first alternates with "look-alike" twins, then with a highly
stylized bucranium. Note that Nr 90 + 132 are from equally
undersized gems.

MSS Nr 59/Frequency: 3/Nr 129 + 92
MSS Nr 60/Frequency: 13/Nr 129 + 92A
MSS Nr 61/Frequency: 6/Nr 129 + 139
This set contains, not "look-alike" twins but a "look-alike"
triad, which does rather compound the sphragistic confusion.
Note this triad's stylistic affinities with Nr 129, the lion-
pawed monster, not least their shared unusual asymmetry. Cf.:
especially Nr 129 upside down with Nr 92:- an elongated
animal head in profile, irregular paws instead of arms rising
on either side of fantail or antler. On stylistic grounds one
would be justified in calling Nr 129 "one of the family".

     This completes our discussion of individual combinations.[18]
In the Variable Combinations (Table 3) no triplets and only
four pairs -- Nr 24 + 112, Nr 21 + 61, Nr 69 + 67, Nr 90 + 132
-- might be found together on a single stone.[19] That means

that, in more than half of the MSS, we can rule out or
consider improbable the use of multifaceted sealstones. If,
as far as we can tell, no more than 24 individuals could have
used such seals, we are hardly entitled to speak of the
"apparent fashion of using two- or three-sided sealstones" at
Zakro.[20] The fashion may be more apparent than real. Of
course, that 38 combinations do not include multifaceted
stones does not mean that the other 24 do not, but it does
sharply reduce that likelihood. On balance, one begins to
suspect that the Zakro gem engravers made normal lentoids,
engraving just one side. If this is is correct, then it was
the use to which these lentoids and, occasionally, other
shapes, were put -- and not the gems themselves -- which was
remarkable at Zakro. Why, then, these combinations?

In an interesting paper some years ago, Maurice Pope
noticed that the combination sealings at Ayia Triada included
four of what we would call Variable Combinations (Appendix I/
Table 1):- AT 40 + 24, AT 40 + 58, AT 143 + 114, AT 143 + 144;
He concluded that AT 40 and AT 143 must have been used to
endorse different seals, i.e. they were countermarkers just as
Linear A inscriptions were, and that they probably belonged to
officials or scribes.[21] Making the same assumptions for Zakro
material, he discovered a minimum of eight such officials:-
seven seal-owners who counterstamped nodules and one whose
seal was found twice impressed on the clay rondel which lay
with the sealings.[22] (This compares with twelve to nineteen
officials who could be variously identified at Ayia Triada.)
The theory is attractive but closer examination does not bear
out its promise. If the Zakro system is built on official
countermarking of nodules, there must be a hidden official in
each of the Variable Combinations, even though we cannot spot
him. This brings our total to a minimum of 37 officials, most
of whom only counterstamp a single seal-type or pair. Worse,
our officials seem almost frivolous in their approach to
business. We can understand only too well Nr 2 who once
counterstamps Nr 62 and once Nr 26 and then disappears for tea
(MSS Nr 34 and 35); what must one think, however, of Nr 21 +
61 who only counterstamps the look-alike twins Nr 28/29,
showing remarkable discrimination in his duties (MSS Nr 49 and
50). In addition, Nr 61 shows himself not to be sufficiently
attached to Nr 21 when he yields his place in favour of Nr 61A,

16

his own look-alike, in the next combination (MSS Nr 49A/50A).
Nr 90 + 132, undoubtedly the most realistic official pattern,
still occupies much of his time with two look-alikes, Nr 33
and 173.

When one examines the overall pattern of stamping and
counterstamping, one is most struck, not by the occasional
variations (the basis of Pope's arguments) but by the sheer
repetitiveness of the combinations. Not only are 33 entirely
invariable, but even some of the variable combinations are
pseudo-variables:- our look-alike twins and triad. The twins
are in each case nearly identical and they must have caused
many an administrative headache in their time. In reviewing
these sets, it is obvious that the interaction of twins or
triad is not only visual; in each case they are counterstamped by the same seal(s):- Nr 28/29 by Nr 21 + 61 (with
the added twist of 61A), Nr 33/173 by Nr 90 + 132, and Nr 92/
92A/139 by Nr 129. When one further considers that Nr 21 +
61 and Nr 129 exist only to counterstamp these look-alikes and
never again appear in our record, one does not think first of
officials at work but, rather, of some tightly welded, closed
entity. They must be either members of the same family or the
same workshop or some similar fixed relationship. It is not
necessary that the seals were made at the same time -- though
they may have been -- but they must have been made consciously
for the same group and made intentionally similar.[23]

Some similar closed group may also be responsible for the
occasional interlocking patterns found in the MSS. MSS Nr 34 -
36 and Nr 51-53 may easily be expressed graphically:-

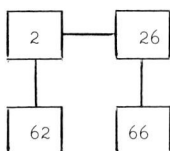

Fig. 1
MSS Nr 34-36

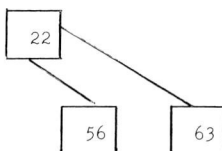

Fig. 2
MSS Nr 51-53

The significance of the patterns may be enhanced by their
iconography:- in fig. 1, both Nr 62 and 66 are Boar Masks; in
fig. 2, Nr 56 and 63 are each linked to Nr 22 by internal forms.

If, as in figure 1, thematic connections are visible, it is
only because of literal doubling (Boar Mask-Boar Mask). But
slightly more sophisticated links may be cautiously postulated
(in spite of note 18!):- where the part may stand for the
whole (e.g. Lion Mask-Lion) or even an imaginative leap (e.g.
Bucranium-Minotaur). Only in the rarest case can we point to
a connection between disparate subjects, e.g. the Boar Masks
and the Running winged figures (MSS Nr 15, 21) but be ignorant
of the reason. We are on slightly firmer ground when, as in
figure 2, the external pattern is reinforced by formal links.
It is unlikely that any but the most superficial formal
connections are haphazard; on the contrary, one suspects that,
in some cases (e.g. MSS Nr 13, 14), the gems might have been
engraved simultaneously while the idea was still fresh in the
artist's mind. The fact that closely related gems are found
together in combination evokes again the idea of "family
likenesses"; what could be more natural than two or three
such seal owners working together?

      Can we extend or explain the "family"? Such relationships
may be clarified by looking at MSS Nr 50 (Nr 21 + 61 + 29).
It must be remembered that this combination was not recorded
by Hogarth,[24] yet it does exist, perhaps more than four times
(Table 3, note 5). Two of the nodules with this combination
were said to have come from Knossos Harbour Town.[25] This
provenance has been disputed,[26] although there is no doubt
that they originated at Zakro, whatever their subsequent
adventures.[27] In my opinion, it is precisely because they
share the unpublished combination that persuades me that these
nodules were indeed Bronze Age losses. Also, they are both
on nodules of triangular prism shape, a shape relatively rare
at Zakro but common at Knossos.[28] That two such prisms were
found near Knossos is suggestive. Can it be that Nr 29
replaces Nr 28 on Knossos business, the "export" branch, so
to speak? We have a hint of such a pattern from Ayia Triada.
There, two sealings found twice in combination (see n. 5 above)
are of the Zakro local monster type:- AT 100 has a strong
"family" resemblance to Nr 51 at Zakro while AT 101 may be of
the same "family" as Nr 80 at Zakro. Perhaps this idea is not
too farfetched:- Nr 80 itself appears on another nodule from

Knossos Harbour Town -- of more normal Zakro shape, however -- which may suggest that the "family" is indeed active abroad.

Returning to MSS Nr 50, Nr 29 is not unknown at Zakro; it appears there twice, compared to 17 nodules with its twin, Nr 28. Such transitoriness is the fate of a "look-alike":- Nr 33 appears 15 times, Nr 173 thrice; Nr 61 appears 18 times, Nr 61A but once; 92A occurs 13 times, Nr 139 six and Nr 92 three times. Though any generalization from a sample of three is out of the question,[29] one might consider either the "export" factor or a human factor (death of one partner?) responsible.[30] In the case of the triad, if one wishes to think sequentially, one might picture two such fatalities in the lifetime of House A's records, not an impossible scenario.

In these three sets, as in most of the MSS, all participants use local fantasy seal-types; no naturalistic types intrude (geometric designs and buildings are assumed neutral in this regard). In fact, it is remarkable how, in the Invariable Combinations (Table 2), almost complete segregation obtains between fantasy and naturalistic types. The few mixed combinations (MSS 9 - 12) seem of ephemeral character. The rest divide cleanly.[31] Variable Combinations (Table 3) are, at first sight, less rigid:- eleven combinations are mixed but, together, they account for only 14 nodules. Thus, it is probably fair to say that the mixed combinations, far from being the linchpins (i.e. countermarkers) of the system, are apparently peripheral. The same cannot be claimed prima facie for the purely naturalistic combinations which, together, total a respectable 78 nodules. One cannot simply dismiss them as foreign to the system or irrelevant. Yet, if we subtract the 37 nodules of MSS Nr 1 -- a signet-signet combination, perhaps of special significance -- the remaining seven combinations look decidedly weaker.

If this is not too extreme a position, we may return to our "family" relationships as being somehow at the heart of the Zakro system. The Invariable Combinations form, then, a closed "family" while the Variable Combinations form a network of "families" often based on pseudo-variations.

1. Hogarth 1902b and Levi 1929b published a total of 405
   nodules with 196 seal-types (plus four fragmentary types).
   After further cleaning at the Heraklion Museum, N. Platon,
   then the Museum Director, identified 33 more seal-types,
   often in most fragmentary condition, some of which seem
   to duplicate previously known types. Photographs of the
   33 types are available in the archives of the Redaktion
   der CMS in Marburg, Germany. A number of Zakro sealings
   are now in foreign museums; most duplicate types already
   known from the original publication. Those in the
   Ashmolean Museum, a gift from the Cretan government to
   Hogarth, were published in Kenna 1960. See also Laviosa
   1969 and CMS xii 174. A few seal-types still seem to have
   avoided scrutiny and these I have assigned consecutive
   numbers 236, 237 and 238. Finally, some numbered seal-
   types appear on further study to be decayed examples of
   other numbered types and these I have either merged (e.g.
   Nr 12/13) or suppressed (e.g. Nr 144 is, in fact, Nr 19
   so Nr 144 is dropped). The number and frequency of each
   number as given in this publication -- though occasionally
   not in agreement with previous publications -- may be
   taken as definitive for all practical purposes.
2. There is, of course, no reason that a single individual,
   as in Near Eastern practice, could not own and use more
   than one seal (I must thank Mr Sinclair Hood for reminding
   me of this possibility). It might be thought that LBA
   burials with numerous rings and gems, though it tells us
   nothing of seal usage, argues for multiple seal ownership.
3. The one exception, which I take as "proving" the rule, is
   the flattened cylinder Nr 119. It is found on six nodules
   with Nr 104 (MSS Nr 3, Table 2) and, again, six times on
   nodules by itself.
4. Categories are not absolute, of course. Humans with
   animals may or may not be cult scenes, for example, or an
   abstract design may be either decorative or fantasy.
5. A few fantasy types, as in the SSS, may turn up anywhere,
   it seems:- six are found at Ayia Triada, two of which
   might even be of Zakro manufacture /AT 100 + 101 in Levi
   1929a:117; see Appendix I/; four more are found at

Sklavokampo /SK 13, 14, 16, 17; see Marinatos 1948: 69 - 96/. The definition of "foreign" must ultimately depend on clay analysis since visual differences may be due to the fire which unevenly baked the nodules or to clay being taken from different, but still local, pits. Still, it is noteworthy that fully 89% of MSS nodules appear slightly orange-red with a few white grits, while only 56% of SSS clay has this appearance; much of the remainder of the SSS is of a quite distinct pale orange clay, either crumbly or powdery in consistency.

6. Combinations found just once in our records include four purely naturalistic, twelve mixed and ten purely fantasy sets.

7. Hogarth 1901: 132-33 described them as "scattered over a small and roughly circular space...." The circle's diameter was approximately 1.2 meters.

8. "Invariable" is perhaps a presumptuous label for combinations surviving in just one example, but it is convenient to treat them under this heading.

9. The shape of the nodules, however, does not absolutely predetermine the number of seal impressions made upon it. Pairs do occasionally occur on three-sided nodules (e.g. MSS Nr 1 is found four times on three-sided nodules; six of the seven pairs in MSS Nr 37 - 41 are on three-sided nodules). Perhaps more surprisingly, single SSS impressions remain solitary though found on two- or three-sided nodules. This suggests that the SSS and the pairs as we have them are complete in themselves and are not truncated to fit the available space.

10. Xénaki-Sakellariou 1958b discussed the distribution of 3-sided prisms and concludes that there is a significant East Cretan bias.

11. Crete in the LBA may be under-represented as the relevant volume of the CMS (Heraklion Museum, Second Palace Period) is not yet published. Still, I made use of the extensive photo-archives of the CMS Redaktion and am reasonably confident that few examples will have escaped the net. A mainland bias seems unmistakable, a bias underlined by the two excavated Cretan example being from a Warrior Grave, Ay. Ioannis, and the Tombe dei Nobili, Kalyvia.

12. Younger 1973: 171-2.

21

13. With the reluctant exception of our first example from the
    Little Palace, Kenna 1962:6 denied that two-sided lentoids
    were ever simultaneously engraved; rather, he viewed them
    as normal lentoids, later re-engraved. Our lentoids 21
    and 22 (Pl. 8 C,D) disprove his viewpoint at least in these
    two cases.

14. Boardman 1970: fig. 80 published this two-sided reel-shaped
    seal. The engraving is said to be rough and the stone's
    surface flat; the gem is certainly not a Zakro original.
    Professor Peter Warren kindly informed me that the stone is
    of a curious blue/black with pale green spots. Reel-shaped
    seals had disappeared on Crete long before the LBA (Yule
    1981: 74 places them, of course, in the Prepalatial period
    but considered that they were in production "at least as
    late as MMIIB.") No contemporary foreign inspiration seems
    at all likely:- reel-shaped seals reappear in post-Hittite
    Anatolia, possibly under Syrian influence, but this can
    hardly be the source (see Von der Osten 1957: 3, 28) What
    the copyist had before him as his model must remain
    speculative, if not mysterious, and the seal considered
    at least doubtful.

15. Levi 1929b: 181.

16. Betts 1967: 20, and Pini 1983 (forthcoming), agree that the
    Zakro ring is "fractionally smaller" than the Knossos
    matrix and related impressions. Betts's theory that
    apparently identical seal impressions found at various
    sites were the work of travelling officials, presumably
    from Knossos, was criticized by Pini in his paper. Instead,
    he suggested that the impressions are not identical but
    subtly different (see n. 22 below).

17. Kindly consult the MSS Catalogue of Combinations for
    illustrations of each example.

18. The reader must naturally wonder to what extent such
    relationships as we have discussed could have been due
    to chance rather than intent. As a control, I ran off
    completely random pairs and triplets. The "Invariable
    Combinations" yielded each time 1-2 literal doublings
    (e.g. Bird-Lady/Bird-Lady), 2-4 parts for whole (e.g.
    Lion Mask/Lion), and 1-2 Lion-Bull interchanges, averaging
    5-6 "meaningful" pairs per run. The "Variables" came up
    with some such pairs but never with meaningful patterns.
    The easiest pattern to reproduce is MSS Nr 37-41, which,

were it not for some stylistic affinities, would deserve
little weight. Stylistic similarities, on the contrary,
are rare in random combinations and almost always superficial (e.g. two winged creatures).

19. We are assuming, however, that, in a system where two-sided
seals are used, both sides will __always__ be used together.
Thus, a seal-type appearing once with one type and another
time with another type is assumed to be wedded to neither.

20. Pope 1960: 202.

21. Pope 1960: 210-202.

22. Pope 1960: 202 n. 7 gives the following countermarkers:-

Seal	90 + 132	countermarks	seal	33
"		"	"	88
"		"	"	173
"	129	"	"	92A, 92B
"	24 + 112	"	"	60
"	"	"	"	105
"	51 + 131	"	"	19
"	"	"	"	144
"	15	"	"	54 + 37
"	"	"	"	59 + 135
"	2	"	"	26
"	"	"	"	62
"	13	"	"	87
"	"	"	"	113.

Relying as he did on numerical combinations alone led him
into some errors:- Nr 51 + 131 must be dropped as Nr 144
is really Nr 19 which makes the Invariable Combination
Nr 51 + 131 + 19; Nr 13 is Nr 12/13 so Nr 75 must be added;
also he has not seen the Nr 28/29 alternation which brings
in Nr 21 + 62 as a possible countermarker, etc. By not
considering sealstone shapes, he misses such countermarker
situations as the signet-signet combinations and others
with mixed sealstone shapes.

23. This assertion has been strikingly confirmed by Pini 1983
(forthcoming) who has shown that the single combination,
MSS Nr 13 (Nr 71 + 89) veils, in fact, six separate seal-
types:- 71A, 71B, 71C, 89A, 89B, 89C, each variant distinguished by extremely subtle alterations; for example,
the variants of Nr 71 are proven by the number of petals

23

in the rosettes on the creature's wings! In such a case,
it seems likely that the artist intended to make identical
seals but betrayed his copies by accidentally changing
such minor details. That the two extra seals were made
for the "family", rather than as forgeries, seems more
than probable.

24. Hogarth 1902b gave Nr 21 + 61 + 28 and, erroneously,
    Nr 29 + 85.

25. <u>PM</u> ii 254-55.

26. Pope 1960: 205 n. 10; Boardman 1970: 99 n. 52 citing
    Pope.

27. Weingarten 1981: Appendix III on the results of an X-Ray
    Fluorescence study proving the Zakro origin of the two
    disputed nodules now in the Ashmolean Museum.

28. Betts 1967: 23-4. In addition to the two from Knossos
    Harbour Town, there are 40 triangular prisms at Zakro
    (7.6% of nodules), all but two of which are in the MSS.

29. But cf.: Pini 1983 (forthcoming) where the three versions
    of MSS Nr 13 (see n. 22 above) break down as follows:-
    71A + 89A = 25 times, 71B + 89B = 3 times, 71C + 89C =
    5 times.

30. It seems reasonable, in any case, to conclude that such
    similar, occasionally almost identical, seals would be
    held by social equals and not, for example, master-
    apprentice or official-layman.

31. The Minoan Genius in MSS Nr 3 would surely have been
    thought naturalistic! I am less sure of Nr 108 in MSS
    Nr 31; Hogarth called it a lion but it looks as
    if drawn from several beasts.

CHAPTER III

ZAKRO SEALING SHAPES AND TYPES

When the moment came to prepare a sealing, the person who actually rolled or moulded the clay between his fingers already had in mind the shape of the nodule which would emerge. This shape was neither arbitrary nor individual but followed familiar and often local conventions. There are six basic sealing shapes at Zakro (see Appendix I for sealing shapes at Ayia Triada and Chania). The borderline between classes is not always distinct. Whether from carelessness or, frankly, lack of importance, variations exist within each class which may further blur distinctions. Nonetheless, since shape may reflect usage, we have made the six shapes our principle classification. The six divide unevenly into two types:- sealings with flat bases, and sealings of prism form.

Sealings with flat bases

Class I (fig. 3)

Nodules shaped like a very thick coin cut off about one-third from the bottom. Both sides of the "coin" are available for seal impressions. The base of the nodules is usually pressed down over a more or less rectangular cushion-shape which may undulate or be smooth. Typically, many deep fine cord marks crisscross this cushion. The nodules are larger than those of Class II.

Class II (fig. 4)

Similar to Class I but with a strong tendency to broaden towards the base, making a triangular rather than straight profile. Generally smaller than Class I but with much the same base.

Class III (fig. 5)

Pyramidal shape with three sides for seal impressions. The base is more or less square. The cushion may be smooth or slightly to sharply undulating, crossed by few to a moderate number of fine cords or , occasionally, a few heavier, twine-size cords.

Class IV (fig. 6)

A flattish, rectangular piece of clay is pinched up on one side. The flat upper surface has space for one seal impression while

the pinched-up side has a generally smaller space for a second
impression (the second impression is, in fact, often incomplete).
The base is smaller but similar to that of Class I and II.

Class V (fig. 7)

The simplest form of a more or less flat piece of clay pushed
down over the surface to be sealed. Nodule may be circular or
rectangular. Only a single seal impression may be made on the
upper flat surface. Bases vary and may be quite irregular and
uneven or may appear much the same as those of previous classes.

Sealings of prism form

Class VI (fig. 8)

Triangular prisms with a "string hole" running through the
centre. Space for three seal impressions. Broken prisms show
inside two ends of the cord which may be knotted together or
simply left overlapping, making the seal itself the fastening.

fig. 3

fig. 4

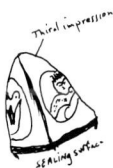

fig. 5

fig. 6

fig. 7

fig. 8

A typological inventory of the Zakro sealings follows.

(27)

MSS Nr	Class							
	I	II	III	IV	V	VI	Other	NC[1]
Invariable Combinations								
1 (10 + 97)	3	18	1	7		3		5
2 (106 + 186/7)				6				1
3 (104 + 119)		1	2	3				
4 (193 + 227)				6				
5 (3 + 102)				1				
6 (154 + 190)			1	1				
7 (155 + 237)								
8 (192 + 238)		1						
9 (164 + 170)	1							
10 (142 + 46)		1						
11 (98 + 20 + 86)			1			1		
12 (196 + 72 + ?)								
13 (71 + 89)2	3	23		5			1	
14 (57 + 73)	2	14		2				1
15 (36 + 64)	5	11						
16 (80 + 134)	5	9		1				
17 (23 + 52)	1	13					1	
18 (17 + 127)	3	8						1
19 (39 + 43)	2	7						

(28)

Variable Combinations — counts table:

Combination					
20 (18 + 83)	4				
21 (34 + 236)	3				
22 (70 + 77)		1			
23 (49 + 130)		1			
24 (32 + 35)		1			
25 (27 + 76)	1				
26 (40 + 50)	1				
27 (55 + 141)	1				
28 (44 + 48 + 78)			18	1	1
29 (25 + 45 + 53)			6	1	
30 (58 + 84 + 74)			1	2	
31 (81 + 82 + 108)				2	
32 (79 + 93 + 111)				1	
33 (38 + 167 + 68)			1	1	

Variable Combinations

Combination					
34 (2 + 62)	1				1
35 (2 + 26)	1				1
36 (26 + 66)	2				1
37 (12/13 + 75)				1	
38 (12/13 + 87)				1	
39 (12/13 + 113)	1			1	
40 (12/13 + 184)				2	
41 (12/13 + 175)				1	

(29)

42 (15 + 37 + 54)			1			
43 (15 + 59 + 135)			1			
44 (15 + 218)				1		
45 (24 + 112 + 60)			5		2	
46 (24 + 112 + 105)						
47 (51 + 131 + 19)			1			
48 (51 + 131 + 85)			1			
49 (21 + 61 + 28)			12		5	
50 (21 + 61 + 29)			1		3	
49A/50A (21 + 61A + 28/29?)					1	
51 (22 + 63)		1				
52 (22 + 56)		1				
53 (63 + 56)		3				
54 (69 + 67 + 30)			1		3	
55 (69 + 171 + ?)			1			
56 (90 + 132 + 33)			10		3	2
57 (90 + 132 + 173)			1		2	
58 (90 + 132 + 88)			27	1	1	
59 (129 + 92)		2			2	
60 (129 + 92A)	2	10		1	1	1
61 (129 + 139)	1	4		1	1	
59/60/61³	1	1				

SSS Nr							
1	2						1
4							4
5							
6					1		
7					1		
8			1	1	1	1	1
9					6		
11					1		
14				2	1		
16					2		
31					6		
41			10		3		
42			1				
47					1		
65		1			1		
91							
94					1		
95					1		
96					1		
99					1		
100					2		

(31)

101		1		
109		1		
110	1	2		
114	4	1		2
116	1	2		
117		4		
118		1		2
119	4			
120				
121		2		
123		1		
124	1	2		
125		1		
126		1		
128		1	1	
133		1		
136		2	1	
137	2	1	1	
140		1		
143		4		
146	1	1		
147	1			
149				

(32)

Value					
150		1			
152					
153					
157					
159					
160	1				
162	1				
163	1				
165	3				
168	1				
172 (+ ??)					
176 (+ ??)					
177	1				
178	2				
179	1				
180	1				
181	1				
182					
183	1				
185	1				
186	1				
187	1				
188					

(33)

189		1	
191		1	
194		1	
195			
198	1	1	
199	2	1	
201		1	
202		1	
217		1	
219			
220	1	1	
223		1	
226		1	
228			
229		1	
230	1		
231			
232			
234	1	1	
235		2	
Misc. quadrupeds	1		

Total	I	II	III	IV	V	VI	Other	NC	
Invariables	28	119	31	32	–	12	2	9	
Variables	4	27	62	3	–	26	2	3	
TOTAL MSS	32	146	93	35	–	38	4	12	360
(% of MSS)	(8.9%)	(40.6%)	(25.8%)	(9.7)	–	(10.6%)	(1.1%)	(3.35)	(100%)
TOTAL SSS	–	10	4	39	93	2	10	7	165
(% of SSS)	–	(6.1%)	(2.4%)	(23.6%)	(56.4%)	(1.2%)	(6.1%)	(4.2%)	(100%)
TOTAL ZAKRO	32	156	97	74	93	40	14	19	525
(% of Zakro)	(6.0%)	(29.7%)	(18.5%)	(14.1%)	(17.1%)	(7.6%)	(2.8%)	(3-6%)	(100%)

1. Nodule too damaged to classify by shape.

2. I have not seen the one nodule with this combination now in the Museo Archeologico di Firenze (= Laviosa 1969: 18).

3. Two nodules with Nr 129 + ? may contain Nr 92, 92A or 139, if not some further variant of them, but their condition does not permit me to choose between the alternatives.

The first conclusion to be drawn from this material is that there are clusters of appropriate nodule shapes depending on the number of seals to be impressed:- Class IV/V (for the SSS), Class I/II/IV (appropriate for pairs), and Class III/VI (appropriate, indeed obligatory, for triplets). Thus, when the same seal impressions occur on more than one shape, the overlap is usually between appropriate clusters. It will be the exceptions to this rule that attract our attention.

Secondly, it is important to note that the shape of the nodule does not absolutely predetermine the number of seal impressions made upon it:- Nr 10 + 97 remains a pair even when stamped on Class III or VI nodules, as do the pairs in MSS Nr 3, 6, and 37 - 41. Equally, the occasional members of the SSS on Class II, III or VI nodules (or, for that matter, the many on Class IV shape) remain solitary even though there is no physical impediment to their taking on an additional seal-type. This suggests that the SSS and the pairs as we have them are complete in themselves and are not truncated to fit the space available. The case of the SSS seal-types on more spacious nodules merely confirms the separation between SSS and MSS in practice if not in purpose.

As a general rule, the person who prepared the nodule for sealing must have known in advance if one, two or three seals were to be applied. Since the seals will have been applied while the clay was still wet, the parties to the event will have been present (which makes it unlikely that the "wrong" nodules for SSS and pairs are mere errors). This suggests, for the most part, a conscious difference between pairs and triplets:- if two seals were sufficient authority, they made up a Class I, II or IV nodule; if three were required, they made up a Class III or VI nodule. Now it may be argued that the Class VI nodule served a different purpose from the others. It is, for example, the only shape suitable for travel. The other shapes, merely pressed down over the sealed object, even if pressed well in, must always have run the risk of breaking off if much handled or jolted.[1] In theory, Class VI might have been available for any seal owner(s) needing its special characteristics but, in practice, only eleven non-triplets took advantage of it. This contrasts with eight non-triplets using Class III which has no physical advantage over their own normal shapes. It is curious,

however, that the pairs making the crossover to three-sided
nodules are all either naturalistic or mixed naturalistic/
fantasy combinations. It is almost as if the presence of a
naturalistic seal changes the rules. Similarly, it is
predominately the purely naturalistic pairs which are found
on Class IV nodules. Class IV nodules are not really ideal
for pairs; the second impression is very often incomplete,
sometimes radically so. Any rigorous system would have
confined Class IV's use to the SSS and, indeed, it may be
some lurking affinity with the naturalistic seal-types of the
SSS that draws these pairs to this Class. Be that as it may,
the fact that the SSS and the MSS overlap on Class IV business
somewhat lessens SSS isolation. It also raises the possibility
that a single SSS-person has the same authority as two or
three together in the MSS.[2]

   We now turn to our study of the sealing imprints and the
fascinating question of what the nodules might have sealed.

NOTES

CHAPTER III

1. The evidence of Nr 80 + 134 on a Class I nodules found at
    Knossos Harbour Town suggests that all shapes probably
    could, with care, travel. Still, it would be most surprising
    if Classes I - V were normally intended for travel. This
    was also the opinion of Hazzidakis 1934: 45 n. 4 who, on
    publishing the three best preserved nodules from Tylissos,
    commented that the nodules which were simply placed upon
    the cords showed that "l'objet scellé n'était nullement
    destiné à être transporté."

2. It is noteworthy, too, that the clay used to make up many of
    the Class IV nodules is visibly very different from the
    rather wide spectrum allowed under the Zakro medium (see
    Chapter II n. 5). Whereas 89% of MSS nodules and 56% of SSS
    nodules are composed of our so-called medium, only 46% and
    18% respectively of Class IV nodules fall within this range.
    This could, of course, be caused by a foreign origin for
    some of these nodules or, more likely, I think, a difference
    in time. We shall return to this possibility in our final
    conclusions.

CHAPTER IV

THE SEALING IMPRINTS

This chapter looks at the question:- what was sealed by
the sealings of Zakro? Hogarth described the sealing imprints
(the traces left in the clay by the object sealed) as having

> a groove on one edge, about /3 mm./ deep and a little
> more wide, scored with straight and oblique scratches.
> This is the impress of something cylindrical, to which the
> nodule was pressed while still wet. The appearance of the
> clay in the grooves shows that this object was not textile
> and it may most reasonably be supposed to have been a reed,
> perhaps a papyrus stalk. (Hogarth 1902b: 76)

The subject rested there for some years. Doro Levi had little
to add when he published the sealings from Ayia Triada. He was
content to illustrate the imprints of just four nodules (see
Appendix I/Table 7 n.) -- two of which indeed resemble those
of Zakro -- and merely remarked that the cord marks or fasten-
ings showed how property was secured in antiquity.[1] Arthur
Evans, while agreeing that property was protected by sealings at
Knossos, felt that most sealings were meant to seal documents,
at least in the later Palace.[2] These documents would have been
written on parchment or even papyrus imported from Egypt.[3] Few
sealing imprints were illustrated, however, and those were of
types foreign to Zakro.[4]

Many years after his excavations at Sklavokampo, Marinatos
noted the apparent identity of seals impressed there and at
Ayia Triada, Gournia and Zakro.[5] This proved, in his view,
correspondence between the centres or, more likely, a chief
cultural centre (Knossos) with lesser provincial towns. He
emphasized that the fineness of the threads which had left their
traces in the nodules proved that only written documents and not
"commercial parcels" could have been sealed.[6] This viewpoint
was adopted by Pope when he studied the countermarked nodules of
Ayia Triada. More than 200 nodules had been found in a gypsum
chest next to the Room of the Graffiti:- if they had secured
jars or storage vessels, some pottery would have survived; if
wooden boxes, they would have been tiny indeed had over 200 been
stuffed into the chest.[7] This, and the extreme slenderness of
the string round which the nodules had been pressed, persuaded
him that they had sealed documents written on perishable
material, papyrus or palm-leaves.[8]

John Betts, who published six plasticine impressions of
sealing prints from Zakro, revised Hogarth's original description. The "groove" was smoother than reed or papyrus stalk;
rather, there was a rectangular object, a pad, perhaps protecting
the object sealed, or a peg or fastener.[9] The "scratches" were
now seen, correctly, to be the imprint left by very fine cords
wrapped around the rectangular object and, thus, similar to cord
marks observed elsewhere. Fine as they were, however, they
could have supported a heavier burden than written documents.[10]

Most recently, Papapostolou, publishing the sealings found
at Chania, meticulously described their sealing prints. He
agreed with Betts's description but argued, nonetheless, that
his sealings had sealed documents, not objects, and were part of
an official archive.[11]

It seemed prudent to return to the source and examine a
larger number of sealing prints in the hope of deciding the
issue. In the Ashmolean Museum I made plasticine impressions
of 28 nodules from Zakro. Then, in January 1982, I was able
to examine the complete body of sealings at the Heraklion
Museum, making plasticine impressions of selected prints. Note
that we are now looking at the positive impressions.

A typical print, showing the smooth object described by both
Betts and Papapostolou, is seen in Pl.27/1. Its smoothness is,
however, misleading. Nearly all examples have, in fact, a
slightly rough texture which can be clearly seen in photographic
enlargement. Furthermore, most such "pads" are not flat:-
their surfaces range from slightly undulating to "wavy" (Pl.27
2 - 6); some are even squeezed out of shape by the pressure of
the cords (Pl.28/7-11). Thus, the rectangular shape is neither
smooth nor rigid (such as wood) but most often rough and pliable.

The outline of the object which was actually bound can
occasionally be seen up to a depth of 4-5 mm.; it may, of course,
have been thicker still. A few nodules reveal an object having
two or more levels, in laminated fashion, as if folded (Pl. 28/29
12 - 13).

The thickness and number of the cord marks vary consider-
ably. Some are no more than threads, but most are about the
thickness of household twine; few would be considered at all
stout. The thickness of the cord does not seem to determine
how well the object needed to be wrapped, for two or three

39

threads were sufficient on some few nodules while veritable
bundles of thread occur on others; the twine-size cords vary
just as much.

None of the sealing prints shows any sign of woven textile
or of wickerwork, or the slightest trace of papyrus.[12] Rather,
the vast majority of prints are of the type we have described:-
rectangular objects, either smooth or slightly rough, naturally
stiff but capable of being cut into small strips and folded.
Leather or hide, strips of which were folded over and bound,
seems the most likely substance:[13] and, indeed, wayward folds
and bulges of leather or hide are clearly seen on some prints
(Pl.29/14 - 18).

Such leather or hide might be thought to have consisted of
thongs tied around the sealed object and further bound horizontally with cords for extra security. Why, however, bother
with the thongs? Why not just tie the object with cord? The
simplest explanation is that the sealed object is itself made
of leather, perhaps a pouch or small bag of some kind. The
natural way to tie such an object is to gather it tightly at
the neck and bind it horizontally; we entirely lack the pleated
folds of a gathered-in neck, so this possibility must be
excluded.

Herodotus (V 58,3) tells us that the Ionians call paper
"skins" (diphterai), a word that was a survival from antiquity
when paper was hard to get and when they wrote on goat and sheep
skins. That the Ionians used parchment is hardly surprising;[14]
that their word for it should be embedded in their dialect is
perhaps significant, for the expression could conceivably reach
back to Mycenaean times (Linear B = di-pte-ra).[15]

Might our sealings therefore have secured parchment
documents?[16] Taking a leaf from the book of medieval parchment
practices shows three ways in which documents were tied and
sealed, any one of which might have left sealing prints such as
those observed at Zakro:-[17]

   1. For closed documents, sur simple queue, a strip was cut
       along the lower margin of the parchment document,
       nearly across to the far edge; the document was then
       folded small, the strip tied round, and the seal placed
       on the strip. This strip has to be cut before the
       document could be read;

2. Sur simple queue for open documents (that is seals
   intended merely for authentication), as many strips
   as needed to carry the seals were cut parallel to the
   lower margin of the document; each strip was secured
   by one seal (or sometimes more).

3. Pendant seals for open documents, tags of parchment
   were passed through cuts in the document, and then
   sealed.

Any of these procedures might have left such traces as are
seen in the Zakro clay, that is, we are seeing the prints of
the strips which tied the documents, rather than the documents
themselves. One important difference remains however to be
explained:- why at Zakro are there cord-marks too? In history,
the switch from papyrus to parchment documents enabled the user
to dispense with cords; the tie could now be made from the
material itself, often cut from the selfsame document.[18] Why
should the Zakro document require both strips and cords? The
most likely answer is that the sealing was made from clay and
not, as later, from wax. Wax is an oily substance which makes
a good bond with parchment, which is itself greasy with animal
fats. When melted, wax enters pores and crevises, and forms a
coat over tiny hairs, a process which helps it to hold when
hard. In contrast, clay is water-based; unbaked, it dries to a
brittle, powdery substance, apt to break at the slightest jolt;[19]
it has no natural affinity for parchment. In order to overcome
this problem of adhesion, it would be practical to fold the
strips over several times -- thus forming our visible lamina-
tions -- in order to provide more surface for the clay to cover,
and then to bind the strips in place and seal. One or two
threads might have been enough to hold the strips in position
preparatory to the sealing; but more threads, even bundles of
threads, would have provided a better grip for the clay:- the
clay could then "bite into" the cords much better than into the
strips alone.

   If we accept that the bulk, at least, of the Zakro nodules
were attached to parchment documents, we seemingly must also
accept that quite a large number of such documents were stored
at House A.[20] It is, however, possible, that at Minoan Zakro
as in Medieval Europe,[21] more than one seal was sometimes
affixed to a document. This solution would fall into line with

41

the Zakro habit of stamping many nodules with two or three seal
impressions. If each combination were a single legal entity,
and not two or three individuals acting in their own right, each
combination that was party to an agreement would have had to
seal the document. Thus, we should, perhaps, not imagine Nr 10
and Nr 97 as two parties to an agreement, but as one, able to
enter into contract with any other combination(s),[22] or, indeed,
with single individuals (SSS).[23] Such a system would halve, at
the very least, the number of documents stored in House A, and
make more manageable the task of the resident scribe(s),
responsible, presumably, for the parchment documents as well as
the Linear A tablet and rondel that lay with the sealings in the
debris of the final fire.

CHAPTER IV

1. Levi 1929a: 71. Prints of the Zakro type:- fig. 2 b,c
   (page 72).
2. PM i 638; PM iv 592 - 98.
3. PM iv 592.
4. PM iv fig. 591, 592; but cf.: PM i 679.
5. Marinatos 1951: 39 - 40.
6. Marinatos did not claim to have found actual traces of
   papyrus, as has been asserted, but assumed from the fineness
   of the cords that papyrus had been used.
7. Pope 1960: 200 - 210. There is, of course, the possibility
   that the nodules were discards, already removed from their
   burdens and "filed" in the chest. In that case, we could
   say nothing about the size of boxes, bags, etc.
8. Arthur Evans (PM i 638, PM iii 423), and many others after
   him, have quoted Pliny and Diodorus on the early use by the
   Cretans of palm-leaves as writing material. This practice,
   so far to the West, seems to me unlikely in any era.
   Rather, I suggest that a conflation of two ideas was responsible for the report:- first that the art of writing
   was invented in Crete (Dosiadas the Cretan, Jacoby, FHG
   iiiB, 458); second that the expression phoinikeia grammata
   was derived from phoinix ("palm"), a speculation that
   possibly came about through hearsay from India where palm-
   leaves were indeed the usual writing-material.
9. Betts 1967: 23. Hogarth's "reeds" should not be entirely
   dismissed, however, as twenty-three of the nodules that
   were studied do exhibit the imprints of something looking
   very much like reed.
10. Betts 1967: 23.
11. Papapostolou: 1977: 13 - 14, 18 - 19.
12. In truth, the most common Egyptian method of sealing
    documents would not have left any trace of papyrus either:-
    a cloth or flax cord was tied around the document and this,
    not the document itself, was sealed. At Zakro, there are
    forty nodules shaped like triangular prisms which were
    moulded around a cord or reed, and these reflect, perhaps,
    some similar system.
13. The same conclusion has been reached independently by Dr.

Ingo Pini, who will publish his results in Pini 1983:
(forthcoming). I am delighted to have his valuable
confirmation on this important point, though we do not
yet agree on its interpretation.

14. The Ionians would have learnt the use of parchment from the
Persians (Diodorus ii 32,4), if they had not already known
it. Parchment or leather was used as writing-material in
mainland Greece by the first half of the 7th century (in
Sparta, Archilochus fr. 81 Diehl).

15. There is no suggestion, however, that di-pte-ra had any
connection with writing. Chadwick 1976: 28 quotes the
Cypriot use of the word diphtheraloiphos ("one who paints
on skins") to describe a schoolmaster, and remarks that
"although papyrus might have been imported from Egypt,
skins of some sort are more likely" as Minoan writing-
material.

16. Writing with ink in Linear A is attested by two inscribed
cups found at Knossos (PM i 613 - 14). I use the term
"parchment" merely to describe a skin used as writing-
material, and not in order to prejudge the probably
unanswerable question of how such skins were tanned and
treated.

17. The sealing of medieval documents is discussed in Kingsford
1920: 19-20, and Poole 1920: 319 - 39.

18. Poole 1920: 323.

19. Perhaps it was the poor consistency of unbaked clay which
led Hogarth 1902: 76 to suggest that the nodules had been
baked "probably intentionally and not by the conflagration
which destroyed the house...." Hazzidakis 1921: 45 n. 4
also thought that his sealings had been deliberately baked,
though he added, not unreasonably, that the purpose of
this procedure was a mystery.

20. Almost 440 nodules, of the 525 which I examined, have
prints like those described in this chapter.

21. Poole 1920: 337; Bond 1955: 225- 226.

22. Variable Combinations would follow the same pattern as
Invariable Combinations, that is, seal as combinations,
but, for reasons unknown, could change their parts. This
might help account for our "look-alikes":- a change of
individuals might not necessarily require a change of parts.

23. The sealing imprints of SSS and MSS are, after all, much
the same.

PART I

CONCLUSIONS

Shortly before its destruction in LM IB, some of the inhabitants of Zakro were participating in a network of affairs exemplified by the pattern of seal usage in the MSS. This network was, at least partly, based on "family" relationships, that is, fixed relationships in which seals, often of slight and subtle differences or variations on a (formal) theme, were used in combination, often repeatedly. We cannot know, of course, if these relations were actually based on kinship (perhaps the oikos) or -- what might in practice amount to much the same thing -- workshops, o-pi or merchant groupings.[1] At the same time, other people were less actively pursuing SSS business. By definition, those of the SSS do not deal (visibly) with each other nor with members of the MSS. The groups are mutually exclusive though their business need not always be distinct.

In the last chapter, we suggested that the business which drew people to House A was expressed in writing, using open or closed parchment documents. To avoid the conceit of near-universal literacy, and to explain the large numbers of documents destroyed in a single fire, we proposed that House A might have housed one or more scribes. In this sense, at least, the business conducted was "official" though not necessarily "palatial".

We have not yet considered why House A was situated at the town's edge, on the northeast hill, on the crown of the lower spur (Pl. 1A, 2A). House A commands the shallow ravine below. With the acropolis opposite, on the higher spur, any traffic moving through this ravine is easily controlled. Such traffic can only be moving in and out of the delta by a mountain road, that is, taking an overland route, perhaps, as suggested by Evans, via Vasiliki to Knossos.[2] In Hogarth's time, a path ran over the acropolis leading, eventually, to Azokeramo on the plateau above (Pl. 2A). In palatial times, perhaps the path ran slightly more easterly to enter the valley between House A and the acropolis. House A, with its imposing Cyclopean masonry, seems ideally situated to protect the low lying palace at this vulnerable point. If so, the mountain road must have

45

been an important route with a significant amount of traffic
moving overland. Taking a more traditional view, let us view
House A as a customs post, a function by no means incompatible
with defense:- none could pass into the delta unobserved or,
plus ça change, untaxed.

The situation and solidity of House A is thus justified by
its function. This also explains why so many people -- as many
as 214 -- congregated there to conduct business:- we suggest
that they were involved in trade and/or the manufacture of items
dependent on this trade. The two sealing systems could be no
more than an indication of two-way traffic:- one, the typical
Minoan SSS, expressing imports while the other, the local MSS,
expresses exports. This is undoubtedly too idealized a view.
It leaves out of account, for example, the various sealing
shapes, and does not explain why some of the MSS combinations
are variables and others invariables, why some are pairs and
others triplets. Yet, it might still contain a grain of truth.
Perhaps those imports (SSS) which were destined for local
consumption, rather than re-export, were distributed to local
artisans (MSS) in House A. Let us imagine, for example, a
textile industry at Zakro, hardly an impossibility. Wool comes
down the mountain from the sheep-rearing plateau to be allocated,
at House A, to local workshops.[3] Finished textiles will be used
at the Palace or sent abroad but some may make the trip back up
the mountain for distribution to other east Cretan sites. We
shall never be able to make all details fit but it could be
that those in the SSS who used shape IV sealings were involved
in a local trade such as wool; as such, they would come into
contact with the shape IV-using MSS. Be that as it may, our
study stresses the local and, possibly, manufacturing aspect
of the MSS seal-users, most distantly related, one would like
to believe, to that winged pair (if not triplet), Daedalus and
Talos-Perdix.[4] This is Eteo-Cretan country and it makes a
pleasant speculation.

Art follows administration, possibly, as once trade
followed the flag. We now turn to the consideration of the
Zakro Master, the analysis of whose work will turn a surprising
light not only on glyptic art in his time but on the glyptic
practices of his fellow townsmen as well.

CONCLUSIONS: PART I

1. On the Cretan _oikos_ as a tenacious unit of social organization, see Willetts 1955: 59-63. On _o-pi_ as textile workshops at Knossos, see Killen 1968 and Duhoux 1976: 83.

2. _PM_ ii 254-55. Unfortunately, we must demolish his most compelling evidence -- that the Zakro-type sealings found at Knossos Harbour Town were made of Vasiliki clay. Our X -Ray Fluorescence study (Weingarten 1981: Appendix II) leaves no doubt that the two nodules from the Harbour Town now in the Ashmolean Museum are composed of the same clay as the undoubtedly Zakro nodules in the Museum. However, we still respect his logical postulation of a Zakro-Vasiliki-Knossos route, avoiding the dangerous sea passage around Cape Sidheros.

3. Along with the wool would undoubtedly come the _di-pte-ra_ of Chapter IV.

4. This may indeed be Talos' legendary country. Apollonius Rhodius (IV 1640) tells that the Argonauts, en route from Karpathos, put in on Crete at Dicte's Haven (identified with Zakro by Huxley 1972: 11, citing Diodorus V 70,6) where Talos kept them off by throwing huge boulders at their ship.

PART II: IN SEARCH OF THE ZAKRO MASTER

L'histoire de l'art nous montre, juxtaposées
dans le même moment, des survivances et des
anticipations, des formes lentes, retardataires,
contemporaines de formes hardies et rapides.
Un monument daté avec certitude peut être
antérieur ou postérieur à sa date....

                    Henri Focillon, _Vie des Formes_: 87

CHAPTER I

PUBLICATION AND APPRECIATION OF THE ZAKRO SEALINGS

One hundred and forty-four seal types were published
with commendable speed by Hogarth in 1902.[1] Nearly all were
illustrated with photographs of casts made from the nodules
and 31 were drawn, often composite drawings taken from two or
more impressions. Hogarth modified the description of one
seal-type, Nr 10, and added a new -- and contentious type --
in 1911.[2] In 1929, when publishing the large cache of sealings
from Ayia Triada, Doro Levi returned to the consideration of
the Zakro sealings. He corrected the descriptions of 34
previously-published pieces and added almost 50 new seal-types
which, because of their poor state of preservation and, perhaps,
rudimentary cleaning, had not been recognized by Hogarth.[3] A
number of Zakro sealings are in foreign museums (see Chapter II,
n. 1); most of these, however, are duplicates of types already
known from the original publication.

Still unpublished are 33 fragmentary seal-types discovered
in the Heraklion Museum by N. Platon, photographs of which are
available at the Redaktion des CMS in Marburg, Germany. Another
four sealings which Platon excavated in the Palace itself also
remain unpublished. I have had the opportunity, however, to
examine all of the unpublished material.[4] Finally, three
interesting seal-types which have hitherto avoided notice --
Nr 236, 237, 238 -- are here published for the first time.

Hogarth divided the sealings into five groups:-

    A. Genre types. Sixteen sealings depicting cult or
        combat;

    B. Monsters and derivative types. 79 examples;

    C. Naturalistic types. 34 seal impressions of
        various animal studies, some of which, however,
        are in non-naturalistic heraldic poses;

    D. Miscellaneous types. Eight examples;

    E. Types not illustrated. Seven examples, of which
        three were reversals of illustrated types and four
        were too fragmentary to justify illustration.

Several of the cult scenes in Group A are of great interest
and have been much discussed in all works touching on Minoan and
Mycenaean religion. The naturalistic types, however, are

generally less satisfactory as art and, with the exception of
a few magnificent bull scenes, are usually passed over in
publications in favour of the excellent examples from Ayia
Triada. It is perhaps not surprising that Hogarth's interest
was drawn to his unique group of monsters:-

> The main object of the catalogue is to show that
> the vast majority of types in Class B are of purely
> local derivation, being variations of a very few types.
> It is a fact to be noted ... that these variant types,
> which seem to have been obtained by the degredation or
> breaking up of others, must have been engraved so nearly
> contemporaneously with their originals that modification
> through unconscious action of the artist, or his want of
> understanding of the model is very difficult to credit.
> (Hogarth 1902b: 91)

Hogarth considered that the variations were consciously made in
order to vary signet-impressions "that might otherwise have
easily been counterfeited or confused."[5] We shall see, however,
that many of the modifications are so minor that confusion
would have been bound to result. And, one would have thought
it _easier_ to counterfeit, not more difficult, seals in which
small variations were always expected. Be that as it may,
Hogarth deserves great credit for recognizing that the bulk of
the monster types flow from a few originals and organizing his
catalogue in such a way as to demonstrate this fact beyond
reasonable doubt.

As one might expect, Hogarth was greatly interested in the
meaning of his monster types. He rejected their having any
religious value:- "these Zakro types do not represent fantastic
gods, still less do they seem to represent priests or votaries
of a theriomorphic worship."[6] He considered them creatures of
pure fantasy, a line generally followed by other scholars.

As far as origins were concerned, Hogarth looked to Egypt,
though admitting the relationships were not very close. His
main evidence, the procession of Nilotic-type demons on a
shell-relief from Phaestos, is not very pertinent and it may in
any case be doubted if these four monsters owed as much to the
Nile as to the Euphrates.[7] The wings of the winged creatures
of Zakro were, as Hogarth pointed out, with but one exception,
not of the Egyptian or Mesopotamian _scarabaeus_ type;[8] the
Zakro-type wing, in fact, only appears in Egypt on the vulture,

an image not otherwise seemingly to Minoan taste.[9] Somewhat disconcertingly, the most obvious analogy for the winged monsters was with fifth century Greece:-

> That fifth century wings should approach nearer to the Zakro wings than do the more archaic ones is to be expected; for the same artistic instinct of naturalism had been at work in Greek art since its renaissance, as in Mycenaean art. (Hogarth 1902b: 93)

The dynamics of this leap past the archaic age were not explained though Hogarth clearly believed in a direct line from the fifth century to Crete via Mycenae. No more did Sir Arthur Evans describe the route though he amplified many of Hogarth's ideas. In particular, he observed that Melian craftsmen were principal participants in the revival of sphragistic fortunes some five centuries after its eclipse and that a variety of winged creatures marked their art:- pegasi, winged goats, lions and sea-horses, Gorgons, and other demonic or semi-divine forms.[10] Not that he considered the Zakro monsters as semi-divine; they are "pure monstrosities and belong to no cult." Nevertheless, he would allow a certain symbolic meaning for such inventions as the butterfly-winged sphinxes and suggested, provocatively:-

> that accidents of artistic invention or of special technique have often produced types to which, later on, mythical attributes have accreted themselves (PM i 707-8)

Possibly such accretions accumulated around the Bird-Lady, a figure of folklore rather than cult, which would help explain her unusual longevity.

Evans added a new dimension, that of aesthetic appreciation, to Hogarth's analysis. Though he agreed that the purpose of the design variations was "born of the wish to baffle forgers of seals ...

> the utilitarian impulse that seems to have been at work was very effective in bringing out the latent ingenuity of the engravers in evolving one type from another. The playful fancy here shown in calling to life mere decorative details, and the daring power of combination ... afford illustrations of the individual spirit and changing moods of the Minoan artists as in no other department of his craft. (PM i 702)

Such combinations, often of the most incongruous elements, led the Italian scholar, Della Seta, to reject any quasi-religious role for the Zakro monsters. They were not even

51

demons, he argued, for they were incapable of living in the
natural world; even those which might have had an organic
constitution show, as they metamorphose one into another
that they lack absolute identity.[11] By stressing the
impossibility of religious content, he, perhaps inadvertently,
underlined the artistic consciousness at work:-

> religion which has created supernatural beings
> follows the conservative principle which is the essential
> foundation of tradition, and fixes the form of these beings
> once for all, and never modifies it.... Religion never
> leaves it to the judgment of the artist to change a type
> fixed by tradition.... This modification is the result of
> a voluntary and intentional design of the artist. (Della
> Seta 1914: 160)

The artist, thus extracted from the mist of prehistoric
collectivism, could now be attacked for his artistic sins:-
lack of Form, lack of control, perhaps even lack of technique.
At a time when the battle against Cubism was all but lost, a
French scholar of the interwar years, D. Isaac, nevertheless
took up the cudgels:- "oeuvres d'une imagination absolument
débridée... d'un esprit utilitaire assez facile."[12] And, for
the coup de grâce:-

> A supposer même que cette aptitude existât chez les
> fabricants de Zakro, comme elle se manifestait à la même
> époque dans de nombreuses oeuvres d'art, il faudrait
> prouver que la volonté de faire oeuvre expressive et
> bien travaillée existait aussi. Or l'examen de l'ensemble
> des empreintes atteste que nous nous trouvons devant une
> production massive, de caractère industriel et, quant au
> dessin, assez grossière. (Isaac 1938: 61)

Another viewpoint of the interwar years was expressed in
scholarly fashion by the Dutch scholar, G.A.S. Snijder. He
diagnosed the artist as having eidetic vision.[13] This condition
is very rare among modern adults but is still found occasionally
in children, primitive races, opium eaters and, by extension,
the Zakro artist. The seals, states Snijder:-

> haben eine ungeheure Realität und sind zunächst
> wohl als persönliche Bekenntnisse oder vielleicht
> "Bannungen" aufzufassen. Wir wissen schliesslich nicht
> annähernd, wozu die Zakrosiegel gedient haben, aber man
> kann jedenfalls mit Bestimmtheit sagen, dasz es ganz
> persönliche Dinge waren.... In ihnen sind uns merkwürdige
> Übergangserscheinungen erhalten, worin optische
> Anschauungsbilder sich mischen, zum Teil miteinander,
> zum Teil wohl auch mit Wahrnehmungen, wie sich dies
> heute noch feststellen läszt bei jugendlichen Eidetikern,
> wobei dann in der Tat mit Augen sichtbar sich die
> "phantastische" Umgestaltung vollzieht. (Snijder 1936:149)

From the low point of Snijder's mystic eidola, the Zakro
monsters did not easily recover. Nilsson dismisses them in
a single, slightly contemptuous sentence:-

> These are the most varying and fantastic combinations
> of heads and limbs of men and animals which seem to be
> the product of an over-heated fever-stricken imagination,
> and of course have no religious value. (Nilsson 1950: 370)

Had a change nonetheless come about? An imagination, however
unpredictable, implies a single mind, a single artist. Most
earlier authors had spoken in the plural, even if only of
"fabricants". Unfortunately, this was not a subject on which
V.E.G. Kenna chose to give a view. On the contrary, in his
major work on Cretan seals, the monstrous elements in the Zakro
hoard were mentioned only en passant; only two such seals were
illustrated, one more heraldic than monstrous.[14] He seems to
suggest that the fantastic and heraldic motifs are at the
expense of naturalism, and that this impending dissolution of
pure naturalism pointed towards the stiff and formal designs
of LM II.[15] As this judgment is of more chronological than art-
historical significance, we shall return to in in our final
conclusions.

Artistic criticism of the Zakro fantasy sealings lapsed
after Isaac. They are not mentioned nor illustrated in important
general works on Minoan art and generally slip from view until
Margaret Gill struck a new note in 1969. The view of a wayward
imagination was updated:-

> He may rather have been a madman, encouraged by
> fellow townsmen in the belief that stones ... would
> acquire from his hand that extra touch of the super-
> natural. (Gill 1969: 91)

We shall leave aside for the moment the tempting equation
between phantasmagoria and madness, and consider her view
of his art:-

> The character of his work can be seen in eighty or
> more surviving designs attributable to his hand or
> influence. By no means incompetent, he deliberately
> exaggerated, reduced or distorted the shapes of natural
> objects, forming monsters from the unnatural combinations
> of their separate parts. In the nightmarish transforma-
> tions that he created, one can see the surrealistic
> working of his mind, in the substitution for one thing
> of another that performed a like function or that showed
> a chance resemblance in shape. (Gill 1969: 91)

Not since Evans had written in 1921 had anyone attempted to understand what the artist was doing _as an artist with an eye for forms_. Distortions and exaggerations need not be due to incompetence, eidetic vision, or even madness, but to the "substitution for one thing of another", a shorthand and elegant expression for surrealism. From this, it is but a short step further to a new critical evaluation which was accomplished, if too briefly, by John Boardman. The Zakro impressions are:-

> from gems which may probably be identified as the work of a single artist, of rare ability and imagination. The devices are grotesques composed of animal and human parts ... with which Hieronymus Bosch could well have felt at home.... The Zakro Master created an idiom which goes far beyond anything we can find again in the history of Minoan, or indeed of Greek art. The technique is perfect.... The reader may judge how difficult it is to study the history of an art which can produce surprises like this. (Boardman 1970: 42)

The artist is now an individual, the Zakro Master, and the continuum of glyptic progress may be interrupted by a single Bosch-like imagination.[16] But how far are we justified in speaking of a single artist to whom all such fantasies are due? Sinclair Hood cautions that the quality of the impressions varies:- some are very fine but others are more crude, degraded or simplified; all monsters therefore cannot be by the same hand.[17] He strikes an important note, too, when he restores the amuletic element, drawing our attention to the possibility that the designs had:-

> some magical import rather than merely reflecting the aesthetic whims of their makers. (Hood 1978: 223)

Finally, Margaret Gill returned to the theme of madness, this time the flowerpower of the 60's giving way to a sterner vision, schizophrenia:-

> In the initial phase of his schizophrenic disorder, the Zakro Master continued to produce competent designs, but they betray his disturbance of thought, or what the medical profession terms "flight of ideas".... As the mental disorder progressed, so the designs became farther removed from their prototypes, until what had started as representational devices were reduced to mere patterns. Even at this stage, he retained his artistic skill, but when the illness advanced still further, the designs disintegrated into meaningless abstractions, poorly executed. (Gill 1982:

This analysis has the merit of attempting to order a sequence in the Zakro Master's work; that it is based, not on a study of stylistic development, but presumed stages of mental disintegration, is unacceptable.[18]

Magic and madness, or art? One hand, or several? If more than one, they could not all, we hope, be mad. If magic, the line between seal and talisman is fuzzy indeed. This study will attempt to answer at least some of these questions. First, we shall try to establish a less subjective method of ascribing work to the hand of the Zakro Master than opinions such as "fine", "crude", or "meaningless abstraction".[19] If successful in isolating the work of his hand, we shall be in a position to study his art as art from an art-historical viewpoint, with at least some degree of confidence. Then, it may be hoped that we can claim some slightly better understanding of seals and seal use in a provincial Minoan town on the eve of the great destructions.

CHAPTER I

1. Hogarth 1902b.
2. Hogarth 1911; the contentious nodule is discussed in Weingarten 1981: Appendix III.
3. Levi 1929b.
4. Since a complete catalogue of the Zakro sealings is already in progress at the CMS in Marburg, this study makes no attempt to duplicate such efforts. Rather, we have limited our attention to those materials and references which may help to elucidate the Zakro Master's place in prehistory. Of Professor Platon's unpublished seal impressions, only one, Nr 218, is relevant to our theme and it appears in its place in the MSS Catalogue of Combinations (MSS Nr 44).
5. Hogarth 1902b: 91, a view echoed by Evans in PM i 702.
6. Hogarth 1902b: 91.
7. That they are in fact of Babylonian origin has been urged by Nilsson 1950: 372 and n.7.
8. The exception is dubious, Nr 49; in our discussion of this seal-type, page 75 , we argue that this is not a wing at all but a helmet's plume.
9. Evans insisted on the ultimate Egyptian origin of the wing, though it may have had to enter Crete as early as the XII Dynasty (PM i 709).
10. PM i 708.
11. Della Seta 1914: 158.
12. Isaac 1938: 58.
13. After he has looked away from a scene, an eidetic can still hold the vision in his mind's eye and transfer it to a blank wall or paper by literally tracing its outlines. Hutchinson 1962: 129-131 is attracted by this theory but, after consideration, rightly rejects it. It is noteworthy that Snijder is the only scholar to attribute some religious value to the Zakro Master's work:-

    Nach meiner Überzeugung hängen sie mit der Religion zusammen. (Snijder 1936: 149)
14. Kenna 1960: fig. 91 and 92.
15. Kenna 1960: 50-51.
16. The Bosch-like quality of his work had been remarked earlier, not surprisingly, by the Dutch scholar, Snijder

1936: 148.

17. Hood 1978: 223; 273 n. 95.

18. It cannot be seemly for two archaeologists to dispute a
psychiatric diagnosis but I disagree profoundly with the
projection of a modern mental concept into the distant
past. Schizophrenia is not a vague term for assorted
symptoms but a set of fairly precise reactions to a given
environment. Since we lack all knowledge of the life and
society of a gem engraver early in the second half of the
second millennium B.C., speculation on his mental condition
must be misleading. The following comments were offered
by a practicing psychoanalyst who is also an art
connoisseur and collector:-

> I do not think it is possible to say that the Zakro
> Master was schizophrenic, nor that he was "normal" (which
> would be far more important). Nor do I think that sur-
> realists today are schizophrenic. In analytic terms,
> they have good access to their unconscious (dreams, day-
> dreams, fantasies, etc.). In a psychotic state, you have
> too much access, too easy, too fast, etc. So, while it is
> possible, once in a while, to have a psychotic surrealist
> (given the talent, technique and determination) the
> psychosis is neither necessary nor even helpful. (Drs.
> M.A. Lombaers, Amsterdam, personal communication)

19. Part of the problem in isolating a "hand" archaeologically
is undoubtedly that a group of artisans may work very
closely together in a single workshop. An individual may
still be identifiable if only by very minor differences;
if not, one has the consolation of having proved an
unusually high intensity of artistic interactions. A
recent study of the problem concludes:-

> in archaeological and historical instances that
> the "individuals" we recognize may sometimes be analytical
> individuals -- our "individuals" may sometimes be more or
> less than one actual person. (Muller 1979: 25)

The reader may or may not agree with my conclusion (in
the next chapter) that there is a Zakro Master but,
though he may possibly be more than one actual person,
he shall not be less.

CHAPTER II

THE HAND OF THE ZAKRO MASTER

This chapter sets out to test the assumption that all fantasy seals are by one hand, personalized as the Zakro Master. Many of the Bird-Lady seals are generally accepted to be by this hand. Taking four of the most characteristic Bird-Ladies -- Nr 20, 23, 24, 43 -- and the closely-related Winged Goat, Nr 37, we shall isolate stylistic features common to all five, the features which combine to make us certain that the same hand is responsible. These factors, or signs of his hand, are listed on the next page. Using the criteria isolated in this manner, we shall then examine all other monster and related seals to determine whether or not the same signs are evident, that is, whether or not our Zakro Master made the seal in question. After a discussion of each seal-type, we shall place it in one of five categories:-

1. Virtually certain to be by the Zakro Master = Conclusion: Yes;
2. Probably by the Zakro Master = Conclusion: Probably;
3. Possibly by the Zakro Master = Conclusion: Possibly;
4. Probably not by the Zakro Master = Conclusion: Doubtful;
5. Definitely not by the Zakro Master = Conclusion: No.

No one would argue, I think, that conclusions 1 and 2 would indicate, at the very least, an analytical individual (see Chapter I, n. 19). Where, on balance, one inclines to his hand, we shall consider it "possible", i.e. category 3; in this category will fall some very interesting specimens. Work which appears to copy his technique and subject, possibly apprentice work, will be "doubtful", category 4. Copies of his subjects, but not of technique, will be "no", not by his hand, i.e. category 5.

Illustrations of most seal-types are given on Pl. 20 - 26; in a few cases, I have only been able to supply my own drawing but all important seal-types are given in photographic reproduction.

SIGNS OF THE ZAKRO MASTER'S HAND

1. All gems are lentoids; all have deep convex faces.

2. Composition is circular, mirroring, perhaps, the lentoid shape of the gems. An imaginary circle would describe head, wings or arms, feet, tail -- nothing would fall outside this circle. The centre of the composition is usually dead centre of the gem.

3. There is a strong contrast between light and shadow indicating that the stones have been deeply cut. Modelling is deep. All forms are <u>rounded</u>. No musculature is depicted. Drill marks are smoothed away.

4. The sense of symmetry is extremely strong. It may well be the organizing principle. Full frontal poses are perfectly symmetrical; even the disturbance of the head in profile is often compensated for by a counterbalancing feature. The top and bottom of a figure in profile will be given equal weight.

5. There is only one subject per gem. There is no background, nor a baseline on which the monster can balance. In a colourful phrase, they "appear to be thrown into the space of the gem." (Della Seta 1914: 159)

6. Movement is linear, either vertical or, as we shall also see, horizontal. Torsion is not used.

7. The monster is supplied with wings or arms, never both. Wings are of the eagle-hawk type with long terminal quills. The upper wing is rounded, not feathered. Feathers fall from the smooth upper wing in neatly drawn vertical strokes. There is no "feathering" effect. There is a fondness for fantails which may either be drawn like the wing feathers or made more rounded.

8. There is a fondness for accessories (necklaces, belts, bracelets, armlets, horns and caps) which also tend to be rounded forms.

9. He has a generous image of womanhood and indeed happily multiplies round breasts beyond nature's intention (we can be sure that his work was meant to be viewed in the impression, not the gem).

59

I. BIRD-LADY SERIES

Nr 20 Dancing Bird-Lady. Sharply inturned legs and pigeon-
toed feet (adorned with anklets) give the impression that the
monster is leaping or dancing. The inward turn of the legs
simultaneously enhances the design's circularity, a trick
repeated on other seal-types. While the feathers on the right
wing are neat and orderly, those on the left wing are more
irregularly drawn, possibly disordered by the violent motion.
The line undulating above the creature's bird-like head goes
on to frame the right wing (the left is lost), possibly intended to restore the symmetry inevitably lost by a head in
profile.
Conclusion: Yes

Nr 21 Bird-Lady with featureless head. Seal impressions are
normally mirror-images of the gems but the Zakro Master avoids
even that affront to symmetry by using a schematic or featureless head. Her head becomes a frontal helmet. Though in the
static position of a displayed bird, her legs are tucked in,
following the line of the flounced skirt, in much the manner
of the Dancing Bird-Lady.
Conclusion: Yes

Nr 23 Bird-Lady with upraised arms. Wings are replaced by
arms, a common metamorphosis, raised at a tight angle, a
feature which will recur in arms and legs on other seal-types.
The feathers now appear on her skirt, a double fantail,
possibly related to the Egyptian vulture's tail. The single
feather emerging from the back of her head may again serve the
purpose of restoring symmetry; it may represent the remnant
of an original bird's crest (cf.: the ivory from Palaikastro,
Pl. 26 F).
Conclusion: Yes

Nr 24 Bird-Lady with plumed helmet. Hogarth was correct in
seeing the object above the aniconic head as a helmet and not,
pace Levi, as part of a gross quasi-bovine head. The helmet
is very deeply cut which tends to make the head fade into the
background in the impression (cf.: Bucranium Series, Nr 81, 82,
86, 87, 170). While symmetry is to some extent lost, the
helmet's plume enhances circularity. Note her jagged necklace.
This is an interesting study of a monster in close-up (note
the realistic enlargment and cut-off of her fantail skirt),

a device which the artist often repeats. If the previous
seal-type might be thought to mimic the goddess with upraised
arms, this seal-type must imitate the nourishing goddess in
an attitude known from Early Minoan times (cf.: Pl. 13 B).
Conclusion: Yes

Nr 25 Bird-Lady with featureless head and fantail. The head
and position is that of Nr 21 but an extremely rounded fantail
(cf.: Nr 53 and 129) is substituted for the flounced skirt.
The jagged belt worn by this monster is the jagged necklace
of Nr 24.
Conclusion: Yes

Nr 26 Fantasy Bird. The centre and bottom of this seal-type
is badly damaged and effectively illegible. Only the wings
remain clear and they are quite characteristic of the Zakro
Master. A new touch is the row of short strokes or "bristles"
along the top of the wings (cf.: the bristles on the wings of
Nr 38 and along the back and throat of Nr 127).
Conclusion: Probably

Nr 27 Breasted displayed bird. Only the pendulous, very deeply
carved female breasts (which quite stand out in the impression)
show that a monster is meant and not a naturalistic displayed
bird. Traces remain of two lines emerging from the back of
the creature's head, perhaps the remnants of a feather as seen
in Nr 23.
Conclusion: Yes

Nr 28 Bird-Lady with fantail head. Four plumes with small
circles between rise from the shoulders of this monster. The
fantail with dots motif recurs on the otherwise unrelated Nr
48. Her wings are slightly hunched up, causing the feathers
to fall in almost vertical lines. The upper wings are smooth.
This monster may be a simplified version of Nr 21 -- a
"family" likeness -- with which it is combined in MSS Nr 49.
Conclusion: Probably

Nr 29 Bird-Lady with fantail head and tail. This seal-type
differs from its close "look-alike", Nr 28, in having more
pendulous breasts which make up half of her body. Hogarth
remarked that it is of coarser work than Nr 28 but this was
not evident in the examples I have studied.
Conclusion: Probably

61

<u>Nr 32</u> Bird-Lady with harem skirt. Although this seal-type is
fragmentary, the monster is breasted and winged in the approved
manner. Her legs are outstretched and she seems to be wearing
a kind of "harem skirt" rather than a flounced skirt.
<u>Conclusion</u>: Yes

<u>Nr 33</u> Bird-Lady Gorgon. Deep modelling and circular composi-
tion preserve the possibility that this over-simplified Bird-
Lady is the work of the Zakro Master (despite its rather gross
wings). Possibly, this is an intermediate monster, half Bird-
Lady and half Gorgon (NB:the eyes and the presumed attempt to
depict a beak in full frontal position); if so, the gross wings
might be a not entirely successful experiment turning Gorgons'
legs into wings (cf.: Nr 44 and 45).
<u>Conclusion</u>: Probably

<u>Nr 173</u> Bird-Lady Gorgon with hairy ears. A "look-alike" variant
of Nr 33; the eyes are more oblique and hairy ears are added.
<u>Conclusion</u>: Probably

<u>Nr 38</u> Seated Bird-Lady. Although the position is new, and
otherwise unparalleled at Zakro, the vigour of the monster --
as if she were about to leap up -- suggests the hand of the
Zakro Master, as does the extremely fine modelling. A single
large breast (she is in 3/4 profile!) is supported by a row of
smaller breasts reminiscent of Nr 23 and 92. Her wings are
folded back (note a faint line of bristles running along the
wings for which cf.: Nr 26); symmetry and circularity are
restored by her extended claws.
<u>Conclusion</u>: Probably

<u>Nr 129</u> Lion-pawed Bird-Lady. This monster is worryingly off
balance although the inward-turned lion-paws attempt to recreate
her equilibrium. This composite creature is based on the design
of a simple triskelion anchored by a characteristic fantail.
The outlined breasts are unusual (but cf.: Nr 90) while her
accessories -- zigzag belt and curved ring -- are orthodox.
<u>Conclusion</u>: Probably

<u>Nr 43</u> Leaping Bull-headed Bird-Lady. A grotesque head trans-
forms the Bird-Lady into a quasi-bovine monster. She wears a
large feather behind her head (cf.: Nr 23). Her legs are the

arms of Nr 23 upside down, and form a connecting link with
Nr 44 and 45. By placing the fantail lower than the feet,
a leaping effect is created.
Conclusion: Yes

II. OTHER WINGED MONSTERS

Nr 34 Running winged goat. This may be the male counterpart
of the Bird-Lady. The winged goat exhibits many of the
characteristics of the Zakro Master's hand:- the wings are
canonical; his horns, though more elaborate than the feathers
of Nr 23 and 43, find there their parallel. He adds, however,
an important new dimension to the Master's art:- his love of
movement turns horizontal and the goat monster breaks into a
run. This is probably the first appearance in art of the
Knielauf (the kneeling-running position) used to depict swift
forward movement. Is it an invention of the Zakro Master's?
See discussion on page 85.
Conclusion: Yes

Nr 35 Goat with skirt. The goat monster of Nr 34 in a more
static pose. He (or she) wears a flounced skirt, from under
which, on one impression, peeps a foot, not unlike the lower
half of Nr 21 in the Bird-Lady series. A transitional figure?
The long circular horn relates this monster to the Minotaurs,
Nr 17 and 18.
Conclusion: Yes

Nr 36 Running winged figure. Unfortunately headless, this
monster wearing a kilt is probably no more human than the
previous ones. In the Knielauf position. His forward wing
is upside down; the smooth wing is below and the feathers
bolt upright; bent at the elbow, too, matching the bend of
his left leg, has the effect of increasing his forward pace.
Curiously, all sixteen examples are broken off at the head,
regardless of the space available on the nodule. Was the
creature always headless, or was the seal broken off though
kept in use?
Conclusion: Yes

Nr 37 Squatting winged goat. Another monster with folded-
back wings; the upper part of the wings is lost so it is not
certain if the upper wing were smooth in the canonical manner.

63

The structure before the monster may be another wing or,
possibly, another appendage intended to create symmetry
(cf.: Nr 38's extended claws). Note how the most ungoatlike
tail, rising up to wingtop, balances the monster and emphasizes the circularity of the composition. His pose is vigorous
and one half expects him to spring forward. The partially
notched horns recur in Nr 39 and 86.

Conclusion: Yes

Nr 39 Breasted goat monster. This may have been an earlier
try in the evolution of the winged goat. It attempts the
springy squat of the previous seal-type but does not quite
bring it off. His balance is still unsure:- the somewhat
coarse and heavy wings tip the creature backwards, a tilt
partly recompensed by the single large breast (cf.: Nr 38)
and the incongruous fore-tail. The long horn is similar to
that of Nr 35; he has, in addition, two feathers behind his
head. The skirt in profile is like that of Nr 38 and,
especially, 32. The composition is strongly circular.

Conclusion: Yes

Nr 79 Monster on haunches. This monster shares some of the
faults of Nr 39, especially the tendency to tilt backwards, a
fault again partly corrected by a tail placed before the monster
(but facing inwards!) and another odd appendage falling from
its nose. Because both examples are broken off at the nose,
one does know know if the appendage continued to any purpose.
The wings are again coarse and heavy but very deeply engraved
and with the canonical smooth upper wing. The creature's
haunches are prominent, out of proportion in size, but very
well rounded.

Conclusion: Probably

Nr 40 Pegasus. Dubbed "Pegasus" by Hogarth, some of the
monster's features -- such as the beak/muzzle, the angle of
the forepaw and the treatment of the hindleg -- are related
to the Zakro Master's work. Engraving, however, is shallow
and the wing structure quite different. A "Pegasus" from
Trapeza Kalou (Heraklion Museum 2643) could be by this same
hand. The "paws up" position of the forepaws is rare in Minoan
glyptic. It is first found on the curious duck-headed griffin
from Thera (CMS v/2 690), then again on a female griffin from
Ayia Triada, AT 99, the Zakro sphinx Nr 41, and the two pegasi.

Conclusion: No

III. FANTASY ANIMAL MASK SERIES

This series, often based on the combination of several disparate elements rather than a single figure as in the two winged series, still illustrates the two cardinal virtues of the Zakro Master's art:- his taste for perfect symmetry and the circular composition.

<u>Nr 56</u> Lion Mask with bird protomes. A strong sense of symmetry is literally reflected in the bird protomes placed above the mask (indeed, the origin of such heraldic poses could have been in the gem engraver's concern to abolish the mirror-image effect between gem and impression). The protomes are deeply cut and well rounded; they are reminiscent of the bird-heads of Nr 20 and 23. Below the lion mask stand two forms -- not entirely clear but possibly based on tusks -- which balance the protomes above and enhance the circularity of the design. The lion mask is well modelled, his bristles neatly drawn. Note his round ears -- the sign of a lion at Zakro, but not the shape found elsewhere on Crete in contemporary lion images.
<u>Conclusion</u>: Yes

<u>Nr 57</u> Lion Mask with waterbirds. His imagination at its most exuberant:- a lion mask (with the round ears of Nr 56) has waterbirds springing from his whiskers, its bristles doubling as their wings to make an organic whole. Above his head, and between the beaks of the birds, is a double axe; the beaks seem to form its shaft. The sides of the axe are very sharply curved so that the tips are long and horn-shaped (cf.: Nr 73). It is perhaps through this chance resemblance to horns, of which the Zakro Master is inordinately fond, rather than to its religious value, that the double axe is incorporated into the design. There is some object, possibly joining the two birds, below the lion mask but the impressions are too damaged at this point to make it out; it, in any case, completes the symmetrical balance.
<u>Conclusion</u>: Yes

<u>Nr 58</u> Lion Mask with wings. An extravagant transformation of the previous type, in which the birds become human legs between which is a "lotus bloom". Below the lion's muzzle are wings

which exactly match the form of the legs above. The Zakro
Master's fondness for wings, however unexpected their presence,
is evident.

Conclusion: Yes

Nr 60 Lion Mask with "snake frame". The lion mask (with
typically, indeed exaggeratedly rounded ears) merges at the
muzzle with a single, thick "snake frame"; the "snake frame"
is transformed, in turn, into indistinct small animals at the
tips. The double axe above the head of Nr 57 becomes partly
incorporated into the mask in the form of a "degraded lotus";
this, in its turn, resembles the featureless heads of Nr 21
and 25.

Conclusion: Yes

Nr 67 Lion Mask with bristly hair. This lion has a very bulbous
head, indeed the only part of him which is obviously non-
naturalistic. A row of more or less neat bristle strokes grows
as hair from the crown of the head. Longer bristles run, as if
in imitation of his mane, horizontally along the sides of the
mask. Though not himself particularly monstrous, he is clearly
from the same hand as the more fanciful Lion Mask Nr 69 with
which it is partnered in MSS Nr 54.

Conclusion: Yes

Nr 68 Lion Mask with round eyes. The head has unusually
prominent round eyes and abundant long hair. The hair rises
on the left of the mask and falls on the right, creating a
circular effect. The long narrow face seems intermediate
between a true lion mask and a boar mask.

Conclusion: Yes

Nr 69 Double-tusked lion mask. Both circular tusks seem to
end in knobbed tips as if identified with "snake frames". The
mask is treated in much the manner of Nr 57. Luxurious hair
growing from its crown suggests vegetation for which cf.: Nr 167.

Conclusion: Yes

Nr 93 Four lion masks. The lion heads revolve around the
centre of the gem but   are not placed nose-to-nose; by
being somewhat out of line, they create a slight circular
or turning movement (cf.: the nose-to-nose lion heads on the
ivory pommel from Shaft Grave III in Mycenae = Karo 295b).
The masks are relatively simplified but have the familiar

tripartite muzzle and bulging foreheads (cf.: Nr 67) as well
as the characteristic round lion ear. Younger 1979: 119
attributes this impression to the Mycenae-Vapheio Lion Master
or his workshop/milieu. If correct, his debt to the Zakro
Master is evident.
Conclusion: Possibly

Nr 59 Boar Mask with wings. The pointed ears of the boar mask
are clear on this much damaged impression. Above the mask rises
an oval form while, below, are the wings which previously
appeared with the lion mask, Nr 58.
Conclusion: Yes

Nr 61 Boar Mask with antennae. The human legs of Nr 58 now
spring from a boar mask, characterized by large triangular-
shaped ears. His tusks balance the composition, rising almost
to touch the legs and complete the circle. Note the two knobbed
antennae for which cf.: Nr 51 and 54.
Conclusion: Yes

Nr 62 Boar Mask with tusks I. A broken impression of a boar
mask with downcurving tusks. The boar's forehead is bulbous,
the cause of which is clearer in the next seal-type.
Conclusion: Yes

Nr 63 Boar Mask with "snake frame". The creature has both a
small set of tusks and, through its snout, a large single "snake
frame" ending in extremely bulbous tips. A staff, with a
bulbous tip, runs vertically through the centre of the mask,
giving his forehead an exaggerated bulge (cf.: Nr 62).
Conclusion: Yes

Nr 64 Boar Mask with tusks II. Variation of Nr 63.
Conclusion: Yes

Nr 236 Asymmetrical Boar Mask. Variation of Nr 64. A very
damaged single impression . The tusks are very long and thin,
longer on the left than on the right which causes an unbalanced
aspect. The creature's snout is more elongated than Nr 64.
Conclusion: Possibly

Nr 65 Boar Mask with tusks III. Variation of Nr 64.
Conclusion: Yes

Nr141 Boar Mask with wings II. Wings rise above the top of his
head on this extremely damaged impression.
Conclusion: Possibly

Nr 66 Boar Mask with small animals. A complicated monster,
seemingly the boar equivalent of the lion mask Nr 60. The
bulbous tips of his tusks develop into small animals topped by
plumes. He has no ears. Two "snake frames" crown the mask.
A "decayed lotus" rises between the tips of the upper "snake
frame", possibly flanked by knobbed antennae.
Conclusion: Yes

Nr 167 Boar Mask with tusks IV. Stalks grow from this head,
paralleling the more leafy vegetation of the lion mask, Nr 69.
Conclusion: Yes

IV. BUCRANIUM SERIES

Nr 81 Bucranium with wings. Very well cut and symmetrical yet
the imaginary outer circle is pierced by the left horn and there
is a taut angularity rather than roundness which makes one
question if this is from the Zakro Master's hand. Note the
repetition of the play in Nr 57 (though an ox-head has no
whiskers):- the wings of the little birds (?) grow directly
from the mask. Two "snake frames" under the ox's muzzle do
not form part of the mask but do rise to touch the bird's wings;
their tips are slightly bulbous. Discussion of this seal-type
on pages 82 - 84.
Conclusion: Possibly

Nr 82 Bucranium with twisted horn. The bucranium is supplied
with normal, but downturning, horns as well as an extra horn
emerging from where a left ear ought to have been; this horn
twists downwards, passes behind the head -- note the play of
perspective -- and returns to view on the right. The tip is
slightly bulbous. The bucranium is not dissimilar to the boar
masks with rounded tusks (cf.: Nr 64 and 65) but the asymmetry
is startling. Discussion of this seal-type on pages 82 - 84.
Conclusion: Possibly

Nr 83 Bucranium with meander. This transformation is based on
Nr 66. The same lower tusks (unfortunately, the ends are
broken off) and small plumed animals emerging, here from the
bucranium's horns rather than from the tusks (if not both).
The place of the "snake frames" has been taken by a meander
with dots (cf.: Nr 49). Symmetry is perfect and, again, a

strong sense of circular composition. Note that the tusks
are in much the same place as the twisted horn on Nr 82.
Conclusion: Yes

Nr 84 Bucranium with loop. A copy (?) based on a variation
of Nr 80 in which down-turned horns replaced wings. Shallow
engraving. The gem was elliptical in shape, not a lentoid.
Conclusion: No

Nr 85 Bucranium with human legs. A very damaged impression
but the treatment of the bucranium's face is similar to that of
Nr 81 and 82. The legs which take the place of horns are related, perhaps, to the disjointed limbs of Nr 92/92A/139 and it
is even possible that this seal is intermediate between the
bucrania and that Stag's head series.
Conclusion: Possibly

Nr 86 Bucranium with wings and cap. Could this be the frontal
view of the running winged figures such as Nr 36? It recalls,
too, the squatting winged goat, Nr 37:- the same thick, coarse
feathers fall from the top of the wing without any intermediate
smooth upper wing; the horn is deeply notched, there partially,
here along its entire length. Even the "cap" on which the
monster rests might be the appendage before the winged goat's
chest (cf.: the position and design of the helmet in Nr 49). The
"cap" and head are relatively lightly engraved (cf.: Nr 24) and
just the wings -- which are symmetrical (the impression is badly
scratched on the right) -- and the horn are as deeply cut as is
the Zakro Master's habit. The face is similar in its features
to Nr 81 and 82. Discussion of this seal-type on pages 82 - 84.
Conclusion: Possibly

Nr 87 Bucranium close-up. This may be Nr 86 brought into
close-up although the notched horns are longer and nearly
encircle the face. Once again, the horns are deeply etched
while the head itself is shallower. Discussion of this seal-
type on pages 82 - 84.
Conclusion: Possibly

Nr 170 Frontal Minotaur. The head of Nr 87 -- the same deeply
notched horns and shallow facial features -- on a human body
graced with animal paws. Discussion of this seal-type on pages
82 - 84.
Conclusion: Possibly

69

Nr 88 Bucranium with snake frames and wheel. A flat featureless bucranium with outlined horns on which are placed two
waterbirds. Above the bucranium are two "snake frames" with
a wheel placed between the tips of the upper frame. The subject
must be from the Zakro Master (cf.: Nr 66 and, especially, 57)
but the treatment is wholly foreign to his hand. Engraving is
generally shallow; even the horns are not deeply cut. The
birds are plumper but they lack any organic relationship with
the horns. The wheel is unique at Zakro.
Conclusion: No

Nr 95 Ox Head. In this much damaged impression, the face
projects rather than the horns but both are deeply engraved.
There is a trace of the typical bucranium features.
Conclusion: Possibly

Nr 165 Bucranium with rosette. A fragmentary nodule, broken
both on the right and just under the muzzle. The head, however,
seems to resemble Nr 81 and 82. On the left is a curved object
which may have continued under the muzzle and ended, symmetrically, on the right; it is difficult to imagine its purpose
but, then, it is difficult to outguess the Zakro Master. The
rosette (?) finds a parallel, not at Zakro, but at Sklavokampo
(see Pl. 14 B).
Conclusion: Possibly

V. BIRD PROTOME SERIES

Nr 52 Opposed bird protomes. Heraldically-opposed protomes
set on a rounded, feathered element which does not seem to be
part of their bodies. From the breast of each bird flows a
serpentine, non-feathered appendage which runs down to enclose
partly the supporting element. A lotus bloom or plumes
separates the protomes (cf.: Nr 58), above which is a thick
fringe of short strokes nearly designing a fantail. Perfect
symmetry, strong circularity, deeply cut. For the naturalistic
treatment of the eyes cf.: Nr 27; for the birds' heads cf.: the
small animal heads on Nr 60; for a more abstract but similar
treatment of bird protomes cf.: Nr 56.
Conclusion: Yes

Nr 53 Bird protomes on fantail. Opposed long-beaked bird
heads (?) are set on breasts above a rounded fantail. Cf.:

fantails on Nr 25 and 45.

Conclusion: Yes

N. 54 Opposed eagle-griffins. These could be close-ups of
the opposed bird protomes, Nr 52. The stiff crests of the
eagle-griffin are already fully developed and built up of
knobbed antennae (cf.: Nr 51 and 61).

Conclusion: Yes

Nr 55 Two birds.

Conclusion: Illegible

VI. MINOTAUR SERIES

Nr 17 Minotaur to right. Modelling is smooth and very rounded;
composition is strongly circular:- the long tail rises almost
to the long curved horn; the same line continues past the nose
to its irregularly-shaped tongue (?). The Minotaur's haunches
are closer to the spread human legs of Nr 45 than to the animal
parts of Nr 79.

Conclusion: Yes

Nr 18 Minotaur to left. A skinnier beast than the well-
foddered Nr 17 but a number of correspondences show much the
same hand at work:- the modelling of the head, including the
exceptional use of drill marks to raise planes, the protruding
tongue, a single curved long horn, and the oddly-placed
pointed ear.

Conclusion: Probably

Nr 218 Squatting Minotaur (unpublished). Fragmentary but
clearly close to Nr 18 (but facing to the right). He is
more in profile and shows just a single upraised arm. Work
seems superficial and probably a copy.

Conclusion: Doubtful

Nr 19 Crude Minotaur. The sole surviving impression shows a
deeply modelled creature with limbs and lines running in all
directions. Design is cluttered, asymmetrical and non-circular.
Most likely a "copy" of Nr 17 but with shallow engraving.

Conclusion: Doubtful

VII. SPHINX SERIES

Nr 71 Butterfly-winged sphinx. The sphinx (is it rightside
up? cf.: Nr 80) is an extraordinary example of the artist's

ability to create new images out of existing elements:- the
lower half of the composition is based on a degraded animal
mask from whose head springs human legs (cf.: Nr 58 and 61);
above, the single lotus bloom of Nr 58 spreads out into a
feathered fantail. Butterfly wings with rosettes are added
and a new monster is born.
Conclusion: Yes

Nr 72 Rosette butterfly. This variation upon the theme of
Nr 71 unfortunately exists in only one poor impression.
Nonetheless, the depth of engraving and the composition both
favour the Zakro Master's hand. That it evolves from Nr 71
(e.g. the pincer) and simultaneously regresses (the lotus
bloom returns) makes it a reasonably certain transformation
from his hand.
Conclusion: Yes

Nr 80 Opposed lion-sphinxes. A degraded animal mask
(bucranium?) inspires still another departure, here picking up
canonical wings and supported by lion's paws. Note the inward
turn of the paws (cf.: the pigeon-toed Bird-Ladies and Nr 129),
a device which adds circularity. A loop tops the head,
simulating, perhaps a single frontal face (cf.: Nr 84).
Conclusion: Yes

Nr 175 Winged warriors. From a fragmentary impression but
clearly another stage in the evolution of Nr 80. The figures
have become humanoid, perhaps two winged warriors face to face.
Conclusion: Yes

Nr 74 Frontal winged sphinx. The animal mask has totally
disappeared, the wings regress to butterfly wings, the lion's
paws remain. She is given round breasts. As is the habit of
the Zakro Master, the head in profile is balanced, here by an
elegant diadem and by several knobbed antennae rising from the
left shoulder (often wrongly drawn as part of the diadem).
Her high wings are balanced by two low rock-like shapes, one
on either side of her lion's paws; could they have been
joined together under her feet?
Conclusion: Yes

Nr 75 Sphinx with head-dress. Though four examples of this
seal-type exist, all are poor, perhaps indicating a very worn
gem. The diadem has become a head-dress; the lion's paws

reach almost to his head. It seems more thrown together than organic. Though displaying orthodox transformations, it is probably a copy of a missing original. This is the only Zakro-type monster standing on a baseline.

Conclusion: Doubtful

Nr 77 A Tergo sphinx. His haunches are smooth and extremely rounded. The wings -- NB: the knobbed ends -- are those of the butterfly sphinxes and Nr 76. Formally, he is close to Nr 70 with which he appears in combination. An extraordinary vision.

Conclusion: Yes

Nr 41 Sphinx I. A sketchy winged sphinx of no particular distinction; may be related to "Pegasus", Nr 40.

Conclusion: Doubtful

Nr 42 Sphinx II. So weakly engraved that one cannot be sure a sphinx was really intended.

Conclusion: No

VIII. GORGON SERIES

The term "gorgon" is used here as convenient shorthand for frontal heads with human or humanoid features, possibly serving an apotropaic purpose. It does not imply any link, mythological or otherwise, with the Gorgons of later Greece.

Nr 76 Grotesque head. The bestial origin of this demon is suggested by his round lion ears; the straight bristles of his hair show his kinship with the animal masks (cf.: Nr 67 and 68). His wings are those of the butterfly sphinxes (note, how-ever, that they do not entirely circle his head but stop on the left, not through a break in the impression, but surely intentionally); cf.: Nr 71, 72 and 74. This monster may be a "close up" possibly derived from Nr 78 through a lost inter-mediary. He, in turn, may be intermediate between the Sphinx Series and the Gorgons.

Conclusion: Yes

Nr 78 Cherub. All but one of the Bird-Ladies with frontal heads had featureless faces, a concession, perhaps, to superstition. This cherub, however, has human features, his eyes and nose carefully delineated. Nonetheless, his animal nature is assured by his round lion ears and straight bristly

hairs (cf.: Nr 76) and the inturned lion's paws (cf.: Nr 80).
The wings run straight across his chest (he has no other body!)
but they are not of canonical type; rather, the upper wing is
indicated by a second, separate row of feathers. In spite of
this development, the rounded modelling -- note the puffed out
cheeks -- and his "family likeness" to other monsters, suggests
the Zakro Master.The shape of his eyes looks very like those of
the Bird-Lady Gorgon, Nr 33.

Conclusion: Probably

Nr 45 Gorgon with fantail head-dress. The spread legs of this
monster are the arms of Nr 23 upside down. His fantail headdress is related to those of Nr 28 and 29. The humanoid
features are not sketched in but are an illusion; the "head"
is, in fact, a lotus bloom.

Conclusion: Yes

Nr 44 Gorgon with fantail. A simplified variant of Nr 45
with the fantail returning to its proper place. Hair is
suggested by thick long bristles and the face reduced to two
eyes.

Conclusion: Yes

Nr 46 Winged gorgon. This gorgon head is more bestial than
human; its length is exaggerated by the straight high plumes
which replace hair. Arms replace ears and his hands turn into
wing-like claws. One could hardly imagine a more explicit
picture of the "warder off".

Conclusion: Yes

Nr 171 Laid-back gorgon. Variation of Nr 46.

Conclusion: Yes

Nr 47 Decayed gorgon.

Conclusion: Illegible.

IX. MISCELLANEOUS MONSTERS AND RELATED THEMES

Nr 22 "Snake Frames". Although true snake frames always have
their tips pointing upwards, this design makes better sense if
they point down. It then suggests, as Hogarth noted, the
dancing pigeon-toed Bird-Lady, Nr 20. If this is an intentional
resemblance, it is very sophisticated art indeed. The Zakro

Master's hand is in any case evident in the rounded modelling and circular design.

Conclusion: Yes

Nr 30 Bow-Coil. Hogarth considered this a distant derivative of the Bird-Lady, the bow-coil being the survival of her breasts. Sinclair Hood suggests, more reasonably, that the upper design is Sacral Ivy of standard type (personal communication). Levi saw the lower forms as dolphins. Be that as it may, the whole is deeply cut and the modelling well rounded.

Conclusion: Possibly

Nr 31 Winged helmet. The elliptical shape of the impression, the a-circular, though symmetrical design, the rope pattern acting as baseline, the flat engraving, all combine to argue against this being the Zakro Master's work. The bow-coil above the helmet and, perhaps, its pleasing fantasy might suggest his influence.

Conclsuion: No

Nr 48 Floral Abstraction. Another example of advanced abstract design:- spread human hindquarters become a tulip-shaped flower with plumes (a lotus bloom?) within. On either side of the flower are small sprays of feathers as if remnants of wings. A meander with dots (cf.: Nr 83) completes the obligatory circle.

Conclusion: Yes

Nr 49 Opposed dog heads. The dog heads are separated by a plumed helmet (cf.: Mycenae gem CMS i 153) built up of a lattice-work headpiece surmounted by a plume with irregularly marked feathers (not a scarabaeus wing pace Hogarth). Although this is the sole example of dogs' heads, they may be compared to the Minotaur head, Nr 17, for similar treatment of planes and rounded surfaces. The plume's rightward curl destroys the symmetry of the scene but, possibly, had been balanced by some object on the broken lower left.

Conclusion: Probably

Nr 50 Fussy monster. Little of this monster remains but the composition seems fussy, with lines running off in several directions. We do not know what, if anything, might have

balanced them. Engraving is shallow but could be the work of
an apprentice or follower.
Conclusion: Doubtful

Nr 51 Lion-headed birds. The back-to-back lion-birds, a new
subject, mark the step where opposed heraldic forms split into
two ostensibly independent creatures. Their relationship with
the Bird-Ladies is shown by their raised arms (cf.: Nr 23),
their fantails and collar necklaces. Each has a knobbed antenna
(cf.: Nr 54 and 61). The crisscross lattice work on their
bodies may be related to the lattice-work helmet of Nr 49
Conclusion: Yes

Nr 70 Palm Trees. Both impressions are fragmentary but the
design is still strongly circular. Treating palm fronds in a
featherly fashion suggests the Zakro Master. It may well be
structurally related to the a tergo sphinx with which it is
found in combination.
Conclusion: Probably

Nr 73 Opposed axe-blades. The plume-like trefoil has an
unusual dotted outline; perhaps it is a close-up of Nr 48
with the dots moved from the meander to drop into the plumes.
Cf.: the horn-shaped double axes with those of Nr 57, its
partner in MSS combination 14. The forms are deeply cut and
the taste for circular composition evident.
Conclusion: Probably

Nr 127 Fat Hog. Hogarth took the hog at face value and thought
it a naturalistic beast. Closer inspection shows it to be more
fanciful:- the absurdly tiny head, with sharp pointed ears and
a frontal featureless face, hardly seems realistic. He wears a
collar of neat strokes around his neck. While an entirely
reasonable row of neat bristles runs along the length of his
back (cf.: Nr 26), another row runs down from head to chest.
Conclusion: Yes

Nr 89 Opposed owls with waz. The sharp pointed ears and
featureless frontal faces of the owls resemble somewhat those
of the fat hog, Nr 127. /I do not insist on the identification
of the species as owls, which is from Boardman 1970: 99; Levi
thought them doves with donkey ears, while Hogarth was more

discreet and called them birds with bestial heads7. The
bristles which ran across the hog's back now form the bristly
outline of the waz. The centre of the waz is filled in by a
lotus, the upper line of which runs around the composition to
end under the owls' feet. The seal is enclosed by a wavy
line unique in Minoan glyptic (perhaps related, as suggested
by Professor Peter Warren, to the bats' wings in Nr 72 and
76). Deep engraving is everywhere evident, especially in the
plump owl bodies.
Conclusion: Yes

Nr 90   Waz-lily. It is easy to imagine this image as a close-
up of the waz in Nr 89. The bristly outline has gone but the
wavy-line frame has moved to become the lower lines of the waz
itself. Still, perhaps the design is too simple for us to be
certain of its authorship.
Conclusion: Probably

Nr 92   Stag Head. This seal presents much the same problem as
Nr 129 in that it is worryingly off balance. True, the head
faces left in partial balance of the heavy antlers. The
upraised arms of dissimilar size cause the whole composition
to tilt alarmingly to the left. Multiple breasts below are
insufficient to weight the monster down. Still, the modelling
is impeccable and the way disparate elements grow organically
one from the other seems diagnostic. The triad of seal-types,
Nr 92/92A/139 are discussed on page 84.
Conclusion: Probably

Nr 92A   Stag Head with straight antler. A transformation of
the preceding type with a straight, rather than curved, central
antler. The left arm has disappeared. In its place is a
balloon-like object which balances a ballooning right breast.
It is still not symmetrical, nor even balanced, but it has a
strong sense of movement.
Conclusion: Probably

Nr 139   Stag Head to right. This is not, as stated by Hogarth,
a reverse image of Nr 92, but rather another transformation.
The head now faces right. The main stem of the antler grows,
not from the ear as in Nr 92, but from the crown of the head
which re-establishes, a bit, stability. The shape of the

breasts in the row below the head falls between those of
Nr 92 and 92A.
Conclusion: Probably

Nr 111   Back-to-back lions. The lion on the left is a good
bit fatter than that on the right, which makes an awkward
symmetry; composition does not seem circular. The lions,
however, are not badly modelled and have characteristic lion
paws (cf.: Nr 80).
Conclusion: Possibly

Nr 112   Gate Shrine. Though a heraldic subject, the lions
have the lion ears typical of the Zakro Master's work.
Modelling is deep; the beasts' haunches are round and well
smoothed. The manes, however, are feathery rather than
bristly (but cf.: the connecting element in Nr 52); the noses
are a single deep drill mark. Still, is it too subjective to
consider it his hand which brings a fresh, and slightly
bizarre note to a stereotyped heraldic scene?
Conclusion: Possibly

Nr 128   Opposed lions beside altar. Unfortunately, the one
impression is damaged. Again, one notes evidence of deep
engraving and fresh imagination at work on a familiar scene.
The lion's manes are made up of very many tiny round drill
marks.
Conclusion: Possibly

Nr 130   Five Towers. A realistic subject removed from reality
by the five round shields below the towers. The shields are
deep and rounded; the towers are arranged symmetrically. The
lattice work with which the towers are drawn is reminiscent of
the helmet on Nr 49 with which it is found in combination.
Conclusion: Probably

Nr 131   Figure-of-eight shields. Badly damaged but apparently
related to Nr 130, perhaps even a transformation of it:- the
abstract, rounded shields support a structure of some sort.
Strong contrast of light and shadow.
Conclusion: Possibly

Nr 104   Minoan Genius spearing bull. The Genius is in unusually
vigorous action, testifying to the artist's interest in movement.
The style and technique, however, are not those of the Zakro
Master.
Conclusion: No

Nr 168 Monster with looped head. Engraving is poor and
shallow, the design unconvincing.
Conclusion: No

Nr 184 Winged lion. An attempt at a naturalistic displayed
bird? If so, a failure.
Conclusion: No

Nr 164 Displayed bird attacked by lion. Shallow engraving.
The bird's wing lacks smooth upper wing and characteristic
feathers.
Conclusion: No

Nr 108 Lion to right. Hogarth considered this a naturalistic
lion but it seems more a composite beast, if naturalistically
drawn. The forequarters somewhat resemble the lion's paws of
Nr 74 and he might sport long bristles as well as horns on his
head. Possibly under the influence of the Zakro Master.
Conclusion: Doubtful

X. SUMMARY OF THE ZAKRO MASTER'S HAND

1. Seal-Types attributed to the Zakro Master

Bird-Lady Series: 20, 21, 23, 24, 25, 27, 32, 43, 224.
Other Winged Monsters: 34 - 37, 39.
Fantasy Animal Masks: 56 - 69, 167
Bucranium Series: 83.
Bird Protome Series: 52, 53, 54.
Minotaur Series: 17.
Sphinx Series: 71, 72, 74, 77, 80, 175.
Gorgon Series: 44, 45, 46, 76, 171.
Miscellaenous: 22, 48, 51, 89, 127.

2. Seal-Types PROBABLY by the Zakro Master
Bird-Lady Series: 26, 28, 29, 33, 38, 129, 173.
Other Winged Monsters: 79.
Minotaur Series: 18.
Gorgon Series: 78.
Miscellaneous: 49, 70, 73, 90, 92, 92A, 130, 139.

3. Seal-Types POSSIBLY by the Zakro Master
Fantasy Animal Masks: 93, 141, 236.
Bucranium Series: 81, 82, 85, 86, 87, 95, 165, 170.
Miscellaneous: 30, 111, 112, 128, 131.

4. Seal-Types PROBABLY NOT by the Zakro Master

Minotaur Series: 19, 218.
Sphinx Series: 41, 75.
Miscellaneous: 50, 108.

5. Seal-Types NOT by the Zakro Master

Other Winged Monsters: 40.
Bucranium Series: 84, 88.
Sphinx Series: 42.
Miscellaneous: 31, 104, 164, 168, 184.
All other seal-types except:-
        Motifs too simple to classify (NC): 16, 132 - 135.
        Illegible (Illeg): 47, 55, 169.

An artist's "handwriting" is never a perfectly fixed
quantity; it varies slightly from day-to-day and, more so,
over time. This is true of any artist's hand, even of any
craftsman's, no matter how traditional his medium or, indeed,
his culture. The Zakro Master's handwriting is surprisingly
clear, its very boldness is one sign of his work. His line
is sure. He has a delicate yet strong sense of composition,
his use of space is beautiful and economic. His creations
may sometimes be accused of a lack of absolute identity but
this is no criticism of his sense of anatomy, which is strong,
but of his choice of subject which is so individual. Certainly,
this choice is part of his handwriting as is his use of many
constantly appearing details and accessories.

It should be obvious that I consider all seal-types in
categories 1 and 2 as by the Zakro Master. Those which fit
most perfectly the signs of his hand as given at the start of
this chapter are easily slotted into the first category. Those
which differ in some small particular(s) -- perhaps the work of
another day, another mood, an idea not otherwise pursued --
but which clearly match his signs in most other respects must
be dropped into category 2. It is possible, of course, that
the second category is the home of an "analytical individual"
(see Chapter I, n. 19) but I do not believe it. Seal-types
which differ in an important particular from the signs of his
hand but otherwise conform, are category 3. To justify them
as his own work requires some discussion which takes place

in the next chapter. I do not think that seal-types of either category 4 or 5 are his work though category 4 might include an apprentice.

It is more than likely that the reader at least occasionally found himself disagreeing with my categorization. I hope, however, that such disagreement was limited to a shift of no more than one level either way. I would consider that any movement of two (or more) levels compromises the purpose of this chapter, that is, to identify more objectively the work from the hand of the Zakro Master. Trusting that this has not happened, and that we are in broad agreement on his work, we may now turn to a consideration of his style and development as an artist.

CHAPTER III

STYLE AND STYLISTIC DEVELOPMENT OF THE ZAKRO MASTER

In the last chapter we concluded that 68 works could be
assigned to the Zakro Master with a reasonable degree of
certainty even if 18 were somewhat less certain than the
others. Another 16 works were more problematic and our qualms
would not let us go further than considering them as possibly
by his hand. Among these sixteen, however, is a series of the
highest quality, the Bucranium Series:- Nr 81, 82, 86, 87 and
170. Accepting that these seal-types are not by the Zakro
Master means the conjecture that a second Master of equal
ability lived, at least for a time, at Zakro too. For his
use of similar subjects and the play of his transformations
demand that he was once in residence and learnt from, or
taught, the Zakro Master. He exhibits, however, an alien
taste for angularity and asymmetry and the use of a mixture
of (relatively) shallow and deep engraving. How likely is
it that a second local artist of such technical ability would
not have betrayed his hand elsewhere? For it is striking
that nowhere else among the Zakro sealings do we find this set
of characteristics.[1] May we not have, in fact, not a second
master, but evidence of stylistic development within the Zakro
Master's own career? Closer study of the Bucranium Series may
answer this question.

Nr 81 and 82 (Plate 23) -- which form, with Nr 108, the
MSS combination 31 -- break the circularity canon of the Zakro
Master's art; Nr 82 is asymmetrical as well. The conception
of the two seal-types is very similar. In both, the vertical
lines of the facial features are stressed to the detriment of
roundness (cf.: Nr 83 whose long bovine face is still created
on round principles). They share the trick of using overlapping perspective:- in Nr 81, the horns are in front of
the birds; in Nr 82, a single horn runs from behind the head
to emerge again in front of the normal horn.[2] This is an
important development for it means that depth may be conveyed
by means other than deeper and deeper cutting (the ne plus
ultra of which may have been reached in Nr 27).

Nr 86, 87 and 170 share, as far as is visible, very much
the same facial characteristics as Nr 81 and 82. It is really

impossible to split up the series; all or none must be by
the Zakro Master's hand. Yet, in these three seal-types, we
find the mixture of (relatively) shallow and deep engraving
seemingly foreign to his hand. In all three, the bucranium
itself is relatively lightly cut; the horns, on the other
hand, are more deeply engraved and, in Nr 86, the "cap" and
wings as well. This development, however, may have already
been presaged in the otherwise irreproachable Bird-Lady with
plumed helmet, Nr 24:- here the helmet is deeply cut while
the head fades into the background (whether the face was
intended to be revealed is doubtful, a reticence I would
attribute to superstition). The bucrania are not as shadowy
as the Bird-Lady's head but the precedent lies there.

Technique aside for the moment, look at the many
similarities between these seal-types and the Zakro Master's
more certain work. In our discussion in Chapter II of Nr 86
we pointed out several major shared features with Nr 37,
Squatting winged goat, notably the same coarse, heavy wings
lacking the smooth upper wing and the notched horns. This goat
is already an advanced type. A possibly earlier try may have
been the altogether less successful Nr 39, the Breasted winged
goat (see discussion of both seal-types in the previous
chapter). If we were to postulate that Nr 37 is the link
between the artist's mature but still orthodox style and a new
experimental period, the Bucranium Series might be explained.
The resulting transformations are blameless examples of the
Zakro Master's play:- Nr 37, Winged goat, into Nr 86, Winged
bull with ram's horns; wings into paws in Nr 170 (the cap,
perhaps, into the large central circle of his skull); brought
into close-up in Nr 87 (the circle disappears and the horns
encircle the head). It is possible that the deep notching of
the horns and the lighter cutting of the heads is an attempt
to add perspective, i.e. forcing the horns to jut out towards
the viewer in the impression (and, as argued in the Signs of
the Zakro Master's hand, paragraph 9, it is the impression
which is meant to be seen). Once such a goal is accepted
bolder experiments may be made, resulting in the overlapping
perspective of Nr 81 and 82. Certainly, the thrust of the
series seems to be a sort of back and forth movement. Compare

Nr 81 and 82, for example, with Nr 83, a fantasy bucranium
absolutely in the style of all other Fantasy Animal Masks.
Nr 83 is wonderfully inventive but entirely static;
perspective gives the others movement, made stronger in the
case of Nr 82 by the asymmetry. This may be the point at
which the Zakro Master's love of symmetry yields to his taste
for movement:- both directions are characteristic of his
work but, in some ways contradictory. They can be reconciled
in the leaping, running monsters but not in the Fantasy
Animal Masks.

Much the same development may be seen in the asymmetrical
triad, Nr 92, 92A and 139 (Pl. 25). Possibly this group has
its origins in a new concern with horns rather than tusks,
the central antler being in each the focal point of the
composition. It is equally possible that it evolved from a
lost Stag Head Series which somewhat paralleled the develop-
ments in the Bucranium Series just discussed.[3] The immediate
impetus may have been through a seal-type such as Nr. 85,
bucranium with human legs. Stylistically, however, it can
only be placed _after_ the Bucranium Series when the potential
movement in deliberate asymmetry was understood.[4] In this
series, a whirling motion is achieved which elsewhere in Minoan
art is created through torsion. Here, one feels the Zakro Master
harking back to a much earlier organizing principle, where the
emphasis is placed on the centre and circumference of the gem.[5]
In truth, the Zakro Master rarely strays far from this ancient
formula (see "Signs of the Zakro Master's Hand, paragraph 2}:-
our triad, from a formal viewpoint, is but an elaboration
of a five-armed swastika. Thus, his most extreme surrealistic
fantasy may have the deepest roots, a conservatism which we
shall have much occasion to point out again.

Through the reintegration of the Bucranium Series into
his work, we are able to follow a possible line of development,
a line which may be expressed as a break from the confines of
his own rules. Though aware of the danger of anachronism, it
is difficult to imagine that this break was not, to some extent
at least, active and conscious. Consider, for example, his
search for dynamic movement.

Minoan artists depicted movement through torsion, the
flying gallop, or, more simply, by separating legs, waving
arms or waving hair. None of these methods was favoured by

the Zakro Master though, as they are used on other gems found
at Zakro, the tricks of the trade would probably have been
known to him. At some point, he must have come into contact
with the oriental _Knielauf_ and realized its potential for
depicting swift movement. This transformation was never
realized by oriental gem engravers to whom the _Knielauf_ remained
a conventionalised kneeling pose.[6] In the 15th century B.C. we
find the Master of Animals in the _Knielauf_ position in Mitannian
glyptic (e.g. Pl. 15 D, E) and it could be from this source
that it made its way to Zakro. It could be for this reason,
too, that the Zakro Master only shows male figures in the
Knielauf:- if his model was the Master of Animals (the Mistress
of Animals was never treated in this way in this epoch[7]) it may
never have occurred to him that his Bird-Ladies could pick up
their skirts and run too. Be that as it may, it is a measure
of his genius that he accomplished the same great transformation
of this pose as, much later, did the archaic Greeks.

The _Knielauf_, of course, only works for figures in profile.
Frontal figures need other means of locomotion. For them, he
seems to have developed a curious but effective pose:- by
pulling legs up and raising knees, he gives them the leaping
movement as seen, for example, in Nr 20 and 43.[8] It is his
unique vision. Equally impressive as an artistic innovation
are his efforts to instil lively energy into essentially quiet
poses. The seated Bird-Lady, Nr 38, seems on the verge of
springing up. We can appreciate this effect most by comparing
her with the (indirect copy?) seated Bird-Lady from Ayia
Triada, AT 102 (Pl. 14C).[9]

Finally, we surmise that these experiments were at least
partly conscious. Possibly unique in prehistory, we see an
artist struggling to attain his vision:- the Breasted goat,
Nr 39, tries to spring but his balance is unsure and the
effort fails; the necessary poise is achieved in Nr 37,
squatting winged goat, who is unmistakably about to launch
himself into the air.

An artist who can be granted such experiments may be
allowed the rather mild experimentation of the Bucranium
Series. If we are correct in placing such seal-types among
his most advanced work, then it seems reasonable to place the
rest of the Fantasy Animal Masks among his earliest. Not only
can we see clearly that _two_ series have been made (cf.: Nr 83

with our so-called Bucranium Series) but the animal masks as
a whole are still static. They are not yet infused with the
vigour learnt from his experiments with movement.

So, too, the Fantasy Animal Masks provide the best link
to the past, to the tradition of gem engraving from which the
Zakro Master may well have emerged. This is the ancient
tradition, especially strong in East Crete, of prism-making.[10]
Lesser artists trained in this tradition may have taken refuge
in the talismanic stone by the beginning of the Late Bronze
Age. It took a signal artist to apply the prisms' principle
of metamorphosis, freshly, to his own fantasy.[11] When we
compare the talismanic metamorphoses of cat- and lion-masks
with the Zakro Master's Fantasy Animal Masks, the one seems
sterile and repetitive while the other lives and evolves.[12]

Similarly, the talismanic artist and the Zakro Master both
draw on the thematic repertory of prism-engraving but, clearly,
each has dipped into this pool in his own way.[13] A traditional
subject which surely must have influenced the Zakro Master is
the horned animal head, most commonly an ox's but also the
mouflon. Popular from the Prepalatial period onward, the subject
lends itself to fantasy treatment even though its basic form
admits of little variation.[14] (NB: All discussed types are
illustrated on Pl. 9). Two early prisms, CS K 9 and K 10,
already have the stylized bucranium's fringe of hair developing
a bristly texture; K 9 also has the downturned horns characteristic of the genre. Types are highly conservative. A prism
from the Mallia Atelier, CMS ii/2 114a, has a similar, highly-
stylized bucranium with double downturned horns (Nr 82 has
bristly hair and double horns, one set of which is downturned).
Another prism, HM 2208, carries the theme further:- the double
horns and the head are outlined twice (cf.: Nr 88, not by the
Zakro Master) and the bristles much exaggerated. The bristles
develop fancifully on the prism CMS xii 162a, not unlike the
meander above Nr 83. They split off entirely on an undated
lentoid from Korakou, CMS v 513; bristles and upper horn float
above the head, somewhat in the manner of the "snake frames"
on Nr 66. Bristles suggest notched horns on another early
prism, CS K 11, a development confirmed on CMS ii/2 120b from
the Mallia Atelier; downturned notched horns occur on Nr 86, 87
and 170. The bull's forehead is a circle on a Petschaft, CMS
vii 34, and on a chance find from Zakro itself, the disk CMS ii/2

86

283; a circle between the horns appears on Nr 170. Finally, an early prism, CS K 19 has a bucranium with a solid structure (branch? plant?) rising from the crown of the skull, a concept which recurs at Zakro (Nr 69, 167). Stylized bucrania continue through the Middle Minoan period to emerge into the Late Minoan age in a somewhat more naturalistic form (e.g. AT 7, CS K 356) but equally in the wilder fantasies of CS K 291 and K 292 and, above all, at Zakro.

Out of the same ancient prism-making tradition may have come the inspiration for such themes as the frontally-viewed human heads, the so-called gorgons. Though not limited to prisms (see next chapter), they are there most common, with a perhaps significant penchant for the 4-sided prisms.[15] One notes especially their early association with wings and wing-like streamers (Pl. 10 A,B,C).[16] Have the streamers some mental link with horns? Compare the gorgons of Pl. 10B and C with the horns of the frontal-facing owl on a green jasper Petschaft CS K 118 (reminiscent, in turn, of the mouflon's horns on the similar Petschaft CS K 119).[17] Is there a transformation from wings to streamers to horns and, possibly, back again? Several gorgons also have bristles for hair (Pl. 10 E,F), and one (Pl. 10 E) even sports the lions' ears so at home in the Zakro Master's repertory.

The early prism engravers may also have given rise to the "monster men". Male figures -- very rarely females -- disport themselves on prisms, either alone or with various symbols, most frequently vases. Very occasionally, the figure breaks out of the conventional stiffness and begins to move (e.g. Pl. 11 A,B) and once -- a unique representation -- to run (Pl. 11 C), a distant ancestor indeed for the rushing figures at Zakro. One may note here, but postpone for discussion in the next chapter, that these males often have, intentionally or not, bird-like heads.

In many ways then we can begin to see the Zakro Master emerging from the East Cretan tradition of prism-making. That tradition may no longer be vigorous, losing ground to the naturalism already presaged at Phaestos in the Old Palace Period. He nonetheless draws on this tradition, manipulates it and, by charging it with his peculiar fantasy, transforms it.

87

CHAPTER III

1. Nor do we find these characteristics elsewhere, not in the contemporary deposits of Ayia Triada or Chania, nor in the occasional sealings come to light elsewhere.

2. Gem engravers rarely use overlapping perspective, preferring to show each figure separately and in its totality. Nonetheless, the trick is an ancient one, dating back at least to the 25th year of Hammurabi where it turns up in Syria (Porada 1957:192; figs. 1,2). Cretan engravers were less inhibited in its use and it is seen occasionally on contemporary seals:- full figures walking behind or in front of an animal (e.g. PM i fig. 363 a,b,c; PM iv fig. 368 a,b); partial overlapping of forms is fairly common in animal scenes (e.g. PM i fig. 503 d, AT 59, Zakro 105) and in scenes of animal combat.

3. Sklavokampo Nr 17 (Marinatos 1948: Pl. iv 17 = our Pl. 14 B) may represent one of this missing series, i.e. a bull's head with stag's horns.

4. If correct, this would virtually deny the sequential possibility suggested in Part I, Chapter II:- two fatalities in the lifetime of House A's records are possible, but less so if all three gems were cut towards the end of the series. Rather, it supports the idea that at least some of the "families" were simultaneously ordered and engraved.

5. That this was the organizing principle of Early and Middle Minoan glyptic was first proposed by Matz 1928: 129-149.

6. Some Late Assyrian gems do move in this direction but that, of course, is later. The pose is discussed in Kantor 1962.

7. It is admittedly more difficult to depict the Knielauf in a skirt (though the Greeks managed the trick). One should keep in mind, as an alternative Syrian source, the griffin demon (e.g. Pl. 15 A,B,C), already a monster. He seems to have vanished before our period, making direct influence on the Zakro Master less likely, but the stylistic dating of Syrian glyptic of this type is now disputed (see Porada 1957: 194; Collon 1975: 197-198).

8. Nr 43 might be thought by some to be squatting rather than leaping but that would make little sense of her fantail.

9. In comparing the two seal-types, one again attributes
    some movement to the deliberate disturbance of symmetry
    in Nr 38. She has her legs tightly folded back under her
    skirt; her wings are also, but more loosely, folded.
    This is balanced by large round breasts and outstretched
    claws but they are of insufficient weight to hold her
    down. AT 102, on the other hand, sits on a "chair"
    (a prop unknown to the Zakro Master); the weight of her
    open wings (copying a lost Zakro original?) is more likely
    to tip her off her chair than let her take off into the
    air.

10. Xénaki-Sakellariou 1958b: 455 emphasizes the East Cretan
    provenance of most prisms, especially those found outside
    excavations. The discovery of the Stoneworking Atelier
    at Mallia confirms her view.

11. On metamorphosis in prisms, see Chapouthier 1932: 186 -
    191 and Chapouthier 1946 but we do not know if an
    individual artist ever applied this principle to his own
    work. At the Mallia Stoneworking Atelier, however, though
    more than one hand is involved (Dessenne 1957b:125 notes
    either a group of workmen or a master and apprentice),
    there is a suggestion of such evolution in a single
    (analytical?) individual's work. Note how the common
    running dog -- e.g. CMS ii/2 87a, 89a, 105a -- evolves
    through 102a, 86b, 113c, into the conjoined waterbirds
    104a and the simple waterbird 91; the design finally
    breaks up in such examples as 125a and 126a,c.

12. On metamorphosis in talismanic stones, see Schiering 1974:
    148 and Kenna 1969: 28 - 31. Kenna 1964: 934 goes further
    and suggests that such fragmentation may be deliberate.
    He also perceptively links this process to such craftsmen
    making new combinations of the fragmentary parts "so that
    the motives remain strangely composite, reminiscent of
    many of the Zakro sealings...."

13. Van Effenterres 1974: 22 - 29 analyzed 350 prisms and
    found the following spread of subjects:-

Human figures (males only)	14.0%
Manufactured items (mostly vases)	8.0%
Insects and fish	7.5%
Animals and birds (especially dogs, goats, bucrania, waterfowl)	35.0%

| Geometric designs | 30.0% |
| Other designs | 5.5% |

The talismanic gem ignores the human form, while the
Zakro Master revels in it. He drops from his repertory,
however, the inanimate designs, not least the endless
vases and vessels; the double axe, popular among talismanic designs, occurs occasionally in his work but only
when incorporated into more elaborate images. Perhaps
the two visions come closest in their treatment of birds:-
the talismanic displayed bird has many of the elements of
the Bird-Lady but is progressively concerned with
abstraction rather than its organic nature.

14. Kenna 1969: Pl. 5 caption.

15. Gorgons in the Pre- and Protopalatial Periods (partly
following Xénaki-Sakellariou 1958a: 80 - 81):-

Vase Painting
Birth-giving goddess from Mallia (?) (Pl. 13 B)
Goblin from Melos (PM i 527c) (Pl. 10 G)
Goblin from Melos (Hutchinson & Eccles 1940: Pl. 19,8)
    (Pl. 10 J)

Sealstones
Imp from Mochlos, chalcedony Petschaft (Pl. 10 H)
Carnelian 4-sided prism, from central Crete (Pl. 10 A)
    Considered by Evans PM i 276 to be a female gorgon
    (but how does one sex a disembodied head?). Note
    its unique protruding teeth.
Steatite 3-sided prism, reputedly from Mallia (Pl. 10 D)
Steatite 3-sided prism, reputedly from Mallia (Pl. 10 E)
Steatite 3-sided prism (highly stylized gorgoneia?)
Chalcedony 4-sided prism, reputedly from Mallia (Pl. 10 B)
Chalcedony 4-sided prism, reputedly from Mallia (Pl. 10 C)
"Grey stone" stamp seal, reputedly from Knossos (Pl. 10 F).

16. Professor Peter Warren suggests that the streamers may
possibly be versions of the wild and long Gorgon hair
(personal communication).

17. Frontal-facing owls and cats may serve a gorgon-like
function for they share with human beings the peculiarity
of staring (their eyes are on a single plane at the front
of the face, and both, being nocturnal beasts, have very
prominent eyes). If the cat on the so-called Royal Badge
of Knossos is more than decorative it may be more
apotropaic than totemic.

CHAPTER IV

THE MONSTER TRADITION BEFORE LMIB

Three main monster traditions appear on Crete no later than the First Palatial Period. First, there are the royal monsters, sphinxes and griffins, both probably borrowed from Syria though their ultimate home was Egypt.[1] Second, the Minoan Genius, whose mother was Ta-wrt, the Egyptian deity, who may also have arrived via Syria.[2] The Minoan Genius is the only monster who unquestionably reached a (semi) divine status, serving the gods in cult.[3] Finally, there are the fantasy monsters, hybrids of every description:- Minotaurs,[4] Goat-Men, Bird-Ladies, and the multitude of creatures who came to flower at Zakro. The first two groups have been much discussed and do not closely concern this study -- other than as background congenial to composite forms. This chapter will discuss only those monsters who might have been ancestral to the Zakro creations.

The Zakro Master's Fantasy Animal Masks almost certainly have their roots in the bucrania and mouflon heads of the early three-sided prism discussed in the previous chapter.[5] That the earlier heads had some amuletic value is likely, especially in view of their survival into the talismanic stone of the Late Bronze Age.[6] Similar extra-sphragistic virtue may be claimed for the so-called Lion Masks which could have been a source, though not the only one, for a number of his works (e.g. Nr 56, 57, 67 - 69). Lion Masks are generally thought strength-giving talismans, an assumption based on their presumed leonine origin.[7] If they had originally been not Lion Masks but Cat-Masks, their purpose may have been more apotropaic.[8] Boar Masks are more problematic.[9] With the exception of one Boar's head in profile, they are absent in earlier glyptic.[10] Yet the subject's importance has been dramatically highlighted by the discovery of a Boar Mask finely incised on a spear head found at Amenospilia (Arkhanes), dating from ca. 1700 B.C.[11]

> Unlike any beast in the natural world, it had the
> snout and tusks of a boar, ears shaped like butterfly
> wings, and the slanted eyes of a fox. (Sakellarakis
> and Sapouna-Sakellarakis 1981: 218)

The Boar Mask presents many points of contact with Zakro creations:- cf.: the "ring nose" of Nr 62, the vertical staff of Nr 63; altogether, it is not unlike Nr. 167, one of the more naturalistic of the Zakro Master's series.[12] This trail, so promising in its religious implications, then peters out for over 200 years.

The first gorgons firmly dated by excavation appear in MM II though, of course, they may be older.[13] We have already discussed gorgons in the previous chapter. Here, we shall only summarize their points of contact with the later gorgons from Zakro. First must come their wings and streamers (Pl. 10 A,B,C,G) for which cf.: Nr 76, 78 and, probably, 33; bristles represent hair (Pl. 10 A,C,E,F) for which cf.: Nr 44, 76 and 78; round lion's ears (Pl. 10E) for which cf.: Nr 76 and 78; a triangular-shaped face coming to a point at the chin (Pl. 10 C, H) for which cf.: Nr 44, 45, 78 and, probably, 33. This is not a negligible list and it seems to point to a persistent, more or less clear idea of a "gorgon".

Still other links are seen in the MMII imp from Mochlos (Pl. 10 H) on a chalcedony Petschaft. His horns may parallel streamers (see page 87 above); between the horns is a knobbed antenna of dubious interpretation. Such knobbed antennae are seen at Zakro, not, it is true, on gorgons but on a number of other monsters, Nr 51, 54, 61 and 66; thus, it might be a feature of monstrous iconography. The imp raises claws on either side of his head; claws and pose are closely paralled in the Zakro gorgon Nr 46. The same gesture and claws are seen on another vase from Melos (Pl. 10 J) and, possibly -- though one does not know if a gorgon is intended -- on a steatite cone from Mallia's Stoneworking Atelier (Pl. 13 A).[14] The Melian figure wears a curious cap, not unlike the scroll floating above the head of his Melian companion (Pl. 10 G). It may be a variant of the streamer; interestingly, the one fits his head rather like the "snake frames" of the Boar Mask, Nr 66, while the other floats in a manner reminiscent of the serpentine line above the head of the Bird-Lady, Nr 20.

Although one doubts that a true gorgon is intended, still less a monster, one must note in passing the remarkable "goddess" incised on a MM I vase from Mallia (Pl. 13 B). The goddess, hands to nourishing breasts, has a completely frontal head, eyes and nose clearly marked; she is in the universal birth-giving position, the position, in fact, of the gorgons Nr 44 and 45. Any connection between representations so

distant in time is difficult to imagine. Perhaps, there were
intermediate steps, one of which might be the female gorgon (?),
possibly also in the same birth-giving position, on the steatite
cone from Mallia (Pl. 13 A).

Male figures appear in the earliest Minoan glyptic, dated
to EM II/III at Sphoungaras and Mochlos,[15] and retain their
popularity as long as 3-sided prisms are made. While it is
difficult to draw a line between distortions due to technical
teething troubles and those intended -- and we do not deny that
the former can lead to the latter -- one fairly suspects that
the bird-like head of the MMIA running male (Pl. 11 C) and those
of his less active counterparts (Pl. 11 A,B,D -- if 11 D is not,
in fact, a prototype Bird-Lady, spawned perhaps by a process of
artistic parallelism). Certainly, this bird-like aspect is
easily accentuated. On a 3-sided prism from Mochos (Pl. 11 E) --
and two more stones from East Crete, all, possibly, by the same
hand[16] -- the line between bird and man is blurred:- the figure
on the left has a fantail while the one on the right has bird-
like claws. In nearby Mallia, the creature evolves into a true
bird-man with human legs, Ikaros's most distant ancestor
(Pl. 11 G). The bird-man is not confined to East Crete; he
appears on a vase from Phaestos (Pl. 11 H).[17] Though the body
is not entirely in proportion, it is not incompetently drawn and
he is clearly bird-headed. He seems to be saluting a large
plant which may suggest some ritual association.

Later (MMII/IIIA), a more bird-like man appears once on
a silver bi-convex disk from the Necropolis at Prophitis Ilias
(Pl. 11 I). He straddles the line between bird and man; the
human element is shown both by his standing position, the tail
merely two long terminal quills as legs, and his arm, which
has a non-avian elbow.[18] Again, he may be connected with a
sacred tree.

The Zakro Master, despite his fondness for winged creatures,
does not develop the Bird-Man. However, two winged goats, Nr.37
and 39, have long snouts which are almost beak-like, which could
suggest intermediate types evolving into, or out of, Bird-Men.

Female monsters leading to the Bird-Lady are also quite
problematic. We can trace for a time a Bee-Lady, a hybrid
unknown at Zakro.[19] Whether the Bee-Lady has any contact with
our Bird-Lady is, alas, unknowable. The Bee-Lady first appears

at Phaestos, in the corpus of sealings dated by their excavator
to MM IB-IIA. Two Bee-Ladies are antithetically disposed
around a tree or plant (Pl. 12 B). Each has a monstrous
head -- a single large eye and bestial muzzle -- and wears a
characteristic curled headdress.[20] Her bee origin is evident
in another sealing (Pl. 12 C):- a bee-monster with human arms
flies among stylized plants:- she has a similar muzzle and
wears the same headdress. Another Bee-Lady, on a lentoid
from Knossos (Pl. 12 A) is more human, perhaps in accordance
with local taste. She can still be identified by her animal
muzzle and single large eye even though the curled headdress
is missing. This Bee-Lady is flanked by a bird and a scorpion,
whether as attributes or merely fillers is impossible to say.
Later, we find a Potnia Theron from Vapheio (Pl. 5 C) wearing
a similar but less curled headdress:- the goddess, her own
skirts resembling a bird's tail, grasps two waterfowl by their
necks. Does she link, or confuse, the Bee- and Bird-Lady?[21]

Another group of female monsters makes a brief appearance
in the MM II period, and one wears a curled headdress very
like that of the Bee-Lady. She is the simian-like dwarf, one
of three from Phaestos and Mallia (Pl. 19 A,B,D). These tiny
figurines, all no doubt originally attached to vases, are
generally considered to be of Egyptian inspiration.[22] In turn,
they may be ancestral to a small group of alabaster and ivory
unguent vases of XVIII-Dynasty date which are connected with
birth-giving (Pl. 19 C).[23] One such vase reached Knossos
Harbour Town to land at the Windmills, near the find-spot of
the three Zakro-type sealings (see page 18).

Finally, there are two clusters of female figures who
might presage the Bird-Lady. They are painted on two vases
from Phase Ib of the Palace of Phaestos (Pl. 12 D,E). First
the famous fruitstand:- in the bowl a "goddess of spring"
rises from the earth to be welcomed by ritual dancers; along
the rim crawl other bent female figures. The goddess and
dancers each wear a headdress -- or have their hair styled --
with four or five rising curls (unlike those of the Bee-Lady
which curl downwards). Their faces are beak-like; they are
shown in profile, each with a single large eye. The crouching
females on the rim have another headdress, a kind of Phrygian
cap, but seem equally bird-like. On the second vase, a "Snake

Goddess" and two cult females (both dressed in hide skirts) have the curled headdresses and beak-like aspect of the ladies on the fruitstand.[24] If such women are the precursors of the Bird-Lady, they evidently have a cult significance which may have been lost by the time the Zakro Master takes up the subject.[25]

Two prisms may link these dancing figures of Phaestos to the leaping Bird-Ladies of Zakro. The first gem, from Mallia, but undated (Pl. 12 F) depicts a further stage in her therianthropic progress:- she is now a long-beaked bird; her arms are well on the way to becoming wings; she stands in the conventionalized dancing pose of the figure on Pl. 12 E. More crudely drawn, and nearly merged with the displayed bird image, is the Bird-Lady on the prism from House C (?) on the same northeast hill as House A at Zakro (Pl. 12 G).[26] Stilted in conception, poor in execution, some such stone may still have inspired the conservative first efforts of the Zakro Master --compare Nr 33 -- a short step in imagination if one had vision.

NOTES

CHAPTER IV

1. The history of both beasts is discussed in Dessenne 1951
    and 1957a, griffins alone in Bisi 1965; only Eals 1973:20
    believes that Syria is the home of the griffin whence it
    moved to Egypt and ultimately, perhaps, to Crete. Griffins
    first appear on Crete in the Phaestos corpus of sealings
    (CMS ii/5 317, 318) as does, possibly, a sphinx (CMS ii/5
    320). A contemporary terracotta sphinx from Mallia is
    described in Poursat 1973 and Detournay 1980: 116 - 118.
    The uncommon "paws up" position of the griffin's forepaws
    (see discussion of Nr 40 in Chapter II) appears on the
    ax-head of Ah-hotep (though at a less sharp angle) and on
    Syrian seals (e.g. Bisi 1965: 73-74, fig. 7); this griffin
    also has the characteristic curl behind his head.

2. Ta-wrt and her claim to be the source for the Minoan Genius
    has been most recently discussed by Gill 1964 and 1970. A
    Ta-wrt scarab from Platanos, with associated MM I pottery
    (PM i 199-200; fig. 148) the oldest Ta-wrt on Crete, now
    finds an almost exact parallel at El Giser, Palestine in
    the first half of the 18th century (Kempinski & Avi-Yonah
    1979: Pl. 12) which might be thought to support a Syrian
    route to Crete. Marinatos 1966:265 emphasizes that Ta-wrt
    is an exception to the rule that the Egyptian pantheon has
    no real influence on European cultures; he ascribes her
    impact to her role in popular religion and, also, in his
    view, to her connection with the calendar.

3. Another monster of Egyptian origin, the Cynocephalus ape,
    may have had some cult significance, though as adorant
    rather than servitor.   Traced back to EM II, the ivory
    seal from Mochlos (CMS ii/i 473), the monster appears from
    time to time (Phaestos CMS ii/5 297) until he expires in
    LM IB (our Nr 5, AT 106); see Chapouthier 1932: 197-199.

4. The so-called Minotaur on a steatite whorl from Ayios
    Onouphrious (PM i 68, fig. 38a = CMS ii/1 113a) is dubious
    indeed and cannot be considered ancestral to LM I bull-men.

5. From the same tradition may also arise the more natural-
    istic bucrania seen at Knossos, e.g. the LM IA (?)
    flattened cylinder (PM ii 619, fig.388) or the sealing
    found in the MM IIIB stratum of the Court of the Stone

Spout (<u>PM</u> i 699, fig. 522), close in style, as noted by Evans (<u>idem</u>) to the Zakro bucrania, though its fantasy elements are more restrained. Perhaps shortly before the Zakro Master began his career, half-fantasy bucrania were in vogue. The rock crystal disk, a chance find at Zakro (Pl. 9E), itself close to the <u>Petschaft</u> bucranium <u>CMS</u> vii 34, may illustrate this background; see also Pl. 9 I).

6.   Kenna 1969: Pl. 5.

7.   <u>PM</u> i 673-74, fig. 492. Chapouthier 1946: 84-87 rightly alters Evans's schema on the lion-mask's evolution (dropping fig. 492c, a schematized butterfly). He then, wrongly in my view, starts the series with the Mallia "gorgon", dated, on stylistic grounds, to MM I:-

a (M.M I)

b (M.M II)

c (M.M.III)

d (M.M.III)

e (M.M. III)

f (M.M. I)

8.   Although lions abound, there are no lion-masks among the Phaestos sealings; there is, however, a frontal-facing horned owl (<u>CMS</u> ii/5 311) for which cf.: the <u>Petschaft</u> <u>CS</u> K 118 and the antithetically disposed owls on a talismanic amygdaloid <u>CS</u> K 225. Compare these and the staring cats (e.g. Royal Badge = <u>CS</u> K 174, <u>CMS</u> ii/2 3, 282) to the lion-masks of Chapouthier reproduced above (n. 7), and to those which survive into the Late Bronze Age on talismanic stones (Kenna 1969: Pl. 6!). See Chapter II n. 17.

9.   Misled by their pointed ears, Weingarten 1981 labelled some Boar Masks "Fox Masks", a misnomer which made more monstrous than need be their fantasy tusk-forms. Pliny <u>NH</u> 8, 228 states categorically that there are no foxes on Crete (supported by the absence of fox bones, a fact confirmed by Miss Sheilagh Wall of the University of Bristol). One could argue, of course, an absence of lions

(and, with one exception, lion bones) did not stop the
Zakro Master from engraving recognizable Lion Masks, but
the history of leonine iconography is long,while that of
foxes non-existent. One could imagine the occasional
import of a lion $\int$ = Boessneck & von den Driesch, Ein
Löwenknochen Fund aus Tiryns, AA 1979: 447 - 449 (?)$\int$,
a royal gift and a boon to artists; importing foxes
strains credulity. Compare the Boar Mask on the Archaic
carnelian scarab (= Furtwängler 1900: Pl. viii 69):-
except for the ears, the type is remarkably close to our
Nr 63 and 167; the later artist is even tempted to
embellish a topknot.

10. Yule 1980: 126; but Kenna 1960: 124 dates the obverse of
the haematite lentoid (K 243a = our Pl. 13 G) to MM III
while the reverse, cow suckling calf, is dated LM I (see
Chapter VI n. 6, below).

11. Sakellarakis & Sapouna-Sakellarakis 1981.

12. Judging from the reproduction, the Archanes beast seems
reasonably naturalistic in conception. Its ears are
indeed too pointed (a failing shared by the Zakro Master's
boar masks), but the eyes are round as would be a boar's.
Compared to Nr 167, doubts as to its species need not
arise.

13. Xénaki-Sakellariou 1958a: 80 considers the history of
the frontal human face and its apotropaic role. See
also Chapouthier 1932: 199 - 201.

14. The position of the body suggests a frontal view and the
protuberances around the head could be some kind of
poorly illustrated headdress. The editor of the relevant
CMS volume, however, considers that the head is in
profile. No certainty is possible.

15. Sphoungaras = CMS ii/2 469; Mochlos = CMS ii/2 477.

16. Mochos = CMS ii/2 219a; Mallia = CMS ii/2 223; Olous =
CMS ii/2 267.

17. An amphorisco from Phase IB of the First Palatial Period
(Levi 1976: Tav lcviib).

18. The excavator, Mr Sinclair Hood, considers it a rather
naturalistic bird perched horizontally above a naturalistic
and horizontal spray (personal communication). The editor
of CMS ii/2 places the image vertically, as seems to make

better visual sense, but fails to note any oddity in its pose or "arms".

19. There is a slight possibility that Nr 38, seated Bird-Lady, is in some way related to a Bee-Lady. If one rotates the photograph by 45° so that her claws point downwards, the reader may judge for himself.

20. The headdress is not unlike that of the griffin which appears at the same time (CMS ii/5 318 but not 317). It may be related to that of the Syrian griffin (e.g. Bisi 1965: fig. 7) or griffin-demon (Pl. 15 B,C) or the Anatolian griffin/displayed bird (Alp 1968: fig. 85, 71). Nothing like it survives in the Zakro monsters.

21. The Lady of Birds is an extremely rare version of the Potnia Theron; one wonders if the Bird-Lady demon confused her role.

22. Detournay 1980: 118-119 and note 5. The figurines certainly have an Egyptianizing look about them. The Mallia example also seems to be by the same hand as the terracotta sphinx (Poursat 1973; Detournay 1980: 117-118, fig. 165) which, however has been "Minoanized" and need no longer look to Egypt for its direct inspiration. One should be cautious, however, in attributing these figures to Egypt as no similar figure has yet come to light in Egypt itself! The hand-to-breast position of a Phaestos example (Pl. 19 B) and the hands-spread-under-breasts pose of the Mallia figurine (Pl. 19 D) are both paralleled in Early Minoan Crete (e.g. rhyton from Mochlos = PM ii 258, fig. 153; rhyton from Mallia = Demargne 1932: Pl. I and II). The only equally early figure from Egypt, an XI-Dynasty clay vessel from Dendereh (Petrie 1900: Pl. xxi = Ashmolean Museum E 1966 = our Pl. 19 E) -- of hands-to-breasts- type -- is of non-Egyptian clay (Murray 1911: 42) and probably had a lid in the shape of a headdress which is against the canons of Egyptian art (idem). The clay of the vessel is equally non-Minoan and it seems most likely that it, and the Minoan figurines, owe their inspiration to a yet unidentified common source.

23. The vases were studied by Brunner-Traut 1970. They depict pregnant women in a crouching position, hands spread below their breasts upon vast bellies (Pl. 19 C).

Filled presumably with the oils or unguents used in
childbirth, some have associations with the birth
goddess Ta-wrt or even Bes (Pl. 19 C). The example
found in Knossos Harbour Town (PM ii 255-256, fig. 150)
is canonical in all respects but one:- a hole has been
drilled into its base, making it into a rhyton. All
the vases are XVIII-Dynasty.

24. That the goddess is presumably the "Snake Goddess" need
not deny her equal association with birds:- at Gortyn,
a cult figurine holds snakes in her hands while a bird
perches close to her cheek (HM 15116); although late,
this goddess-figure shows that the dual association is
known.

25. Such "demythologizing" may turn out to be more the rule
than Evans's accretion of mythical attributes (PM i 707),
at least as concerns the Bird-Man and Bird-Lady. This
loss of religious value may be analogous to that of the
nymphs.

26. Probably the "three-sided steatite lentoid of poor and
late work" picked up on the surface of the soil above
the cellar in House C (Hogarth 1901: 134). See also
the editor's remarks in CMS ii/2 381.

CHAPTER V

FOREIGN INFLUENCE, A SUGGESTION

We have already discussed one area where the Zakro Master
must have come into contact with a foreign idea:- in his
adaptation of the oriental Knielauf (p. 85). Independent
invention can never be entirely ruled out, of course, but
given the close relations between Zakro and Syria at this time,
the arrival at Zakro of an oriental seal or ivory carving with
this pose is prima facie more likely.[1] A second area of
received influence is more problematic:- may the Zakro Master
have been inspired in his Bird-Ladies and other dancing winged
figures by the Egyptian god Bes?[2]

Egyptian Bes was in every sense a popular god and his
service spread to Syria and Palestine no later than the
beginning of the New Kingdom. Bes is a lion-headed, bow-legged
dwarf god usually pictured -- almost uniquely so in Egyptian
art -- full-faced rather than in profile (Pl. 16-18). He is
monstrous, grinning, terrifying. From the time of the Middle
Kingdom onwards, he is worn on amulets because of his multifaceted apotropaic functions (Pl. 18 B,D,E). His stare drives
off evil spirits; he provides protection -- he often holds
the SA sign -- especially for children. With the hippopotamus
goddess, Ta-wrt, he serves as protective spirit of childbirth
(Pl. 16A, 17A). The "Serpent-Biter" (Pl. 16 B,D, 17C, 18A),
Bes destroys snakes; he demonstrates this power directly
(Pl. 18 C) or through music (Pl. 17 D). More generally, Bes
also watches over music and dancing -- as such, an unusually
lively figures in Egyptian art (Pl. 17 B,D, 18 F)[5] -- the din
and movements contributing to his prophylactic purpose.

The iconography of Bes is varied, far more a composite
picture made up of shifting elements than a divinely ordained
image. Typically, his face has thick leonine features, lion's
ears, a heavy mane, beard and mustache; his tongue hangs down
like a Gorgon's (Pl. 17 A,B,C). He may wear a lion skin or,
more often, a Syrian kilt. His headdress is usually made up
of upright feathers, reminiscent, perhaps, of his African
origin. When pictured frontally, he is almost always squat
and bow-legged, a feature which gives him a surprising air of
vertical movement. He is sometimes winged, more commonly in

101

Syria but also in Egypt. Although male, Bes is occasionally pictured with pendulous female breasts, a sign of his fecund nature (Pl. 16 A,C,E, 17 E, 18 A,C).[6] By Egyptian standards, Bes is an unusually "seamless" monster, the human and bestial elements mixing in a harmonious whole.

The similarities between Bes and some Zakro monsters are striking:- frontal face, feathered headdress, lion ears, wings, breasts on winged composite monsters.[7] Equally important is Bes's sense of movement. Bes, with musical instruments or in dance, is quite lively. Even standing still, however, his bent legs give him a slight feeling of vertical movement, i.e. leaping. This seems quite unintentional, potential rather than realized, but that would not inhibit the Zakro Master from seizing upon this feature and transforming it as he transformed the Knielauf. May we not have here the inspiration for the curious leaping pose we mentioned earlier (p. 87):- legs up, knees raised as in Nr 20 and 43?

Possibly, too, the Zakro Master misunderstood the function of female breasts on Bes, interpreting him as a female spirit (the more readily as Bes is a spirit protecting childbirth, often a female role); he then went on to endow his creations with the rather ampler, Minoan-scale breasts appropriate to his vision. One does not suppose that the Zakro Master ever copied an Egyptian or Syrian model, even if he had it at first hand, but rather absorbed the Bes vocabulary into his own repertory for reuse in novel ways. The upraised arms of a Bes figure (e.g. 18 C or E), for example, may have been taken over by the Bird-Lady, Nr 23, but no other feature of Bes is simultaneously incorporated.

Have we any proof of this process? No Bes figure has ever been found in prehistoric Crete.[8] This matters, however, less with Bes than it would in most other cases for, such were Bes's prophylactic powers, that he was often tattooed on women (e.g. Schneider 1981: Nr 14; our Pl. 19 C reflects this habit). There is a suggestion that the Zakro Master understood something of Bes and that he himself could further develop the theme. The Bird-Lady, Nr 43, and the gorgons, Nr 44, 45, 46 and 171, have the spread legs of the unmistakable, universal childbearing position. Bes, though a spirit of childbirth, is

never pictured in this way -- for the obvious reason that he
is male. But, at Zakro, it is as if the artist has extended
the iconographic range in a _logical_ manner:- protector of
childbirth in childbearing pose -- and created the appropriate
image.[9]

If so, we must reconsider the purpose of the Zakro
Master's seals. We know that they served a sphragistic
purpose, but had they also -- as the Bes image always had --
some amuletic power?[10] The line between amulet and seal is
not always clear.[11] Yet, if we are correct that the Bird-Lady
is at least partly a transformation of Bes and that Bes is
behind the frontal-facing gorgons in childbearing pose -- two
intensely powerful images combined -- this suggests rather
more than a secondary amuletic purpose.

When we recall:-

-- that most of the Zakro Master's seals are used in the
   MSS and few in the SSS,
-- that the divide between MSS and SSS is all but absolute,
   implying that it is based on some absolute distinction,
-- that the MSS has a pronounced local character,
-- that the MSS is virtually a closed system, based, to
   some extent, on "family likenesses",
-- that there is a hint that SSS seal-owners exercise
   more authority on their own

we may at least entertain the idea that most, but not
necessarily all, of the Zakro Master's seals were carried by
women.[12]

If women are involved, the industry expressed by the MSS
system at least, most probably is concerned with textiles,
the one industry in which women may well have played a major
role.[13] As we have left Bes far behind, however, we shall
postpone further speculations on this theme for our general
conclusions.

NOTES

CHAPTER V

1. Cretan seal engravers were possibly working in Syria at
   Amorite courts from the late seventeenth century onwards
   and it is possible that one brought the pose home with
   him (see Buchanan 1966: 166-167; and Seyrig 1955).

2. On the god Bes, most recently Padró i Parcerisa 1978;
   Wilson 1975; earlier but still valuable studies are
   Weybrouck 1939 and Ballod 1913.

3. Marinatos's observation (see Chapter IV, n.2) that it was
   the popular deity Ta-wrt who was adopted into Minoan
   culture might serve to explain Bes's advent as well.

4. Altenmüller 1964 on his early apotropaic history. Depicted
   at the birth of Hatschepsut (Naville 1908: Pl. 52), thus
   within the XVII-Dynasty, Bes remains the patron of royal
   birth throughout the New Kingdom, especially after his
   boost by the daughter of Amenophis III, Sat-Amen. Though
   raised to such eminence, Bes is nonetheless pre-eminently
   popular and his amulets, found in immense number, are worn
   by all classes (Pl. 18 D, for example, shows Bes worn by
   a slave girl).

5. Davis 1907: 40 observes, however, that our Plate 17 B
   (dated ca. 1400 B.C.) may itself owe its special liveliness
   to foreign influence.

6. Ward 1972 notes that male Bes is illustrated with female
   breasts from at least XVIII-Dynasty but that the female
   Bes, Beset, is no earlier than Ptolemaic.

7. But, equally, note certain obvious differences:- lack of
   knives, musical instruments or other Bes attributes; lack
   of typical leonine face (but note the lion's ears on the
   gorgons, Nr 46 and 48!); no beard or lolling tongue.

8. There is a hint of an earlier Bes arrival in the Aegean
   in the famous gold pendant from the Aegina Treasure
   where the frontal facing head and plumed headdress might
   signal a local adaptation of Bes. Also the frontal-facing
   heads on a gold jewel pendant seen on a MM III fresco
   (PM i fig. 383) could owe something to Bes's inspiration.

9. An image, perhaps, with ancient Minoan sanction (e.g.
   Pl. 13 A,B).

10. Gill 1969: 91 and again 1981:86 suggests an added power

due to the artist's madness; Hood 1978: 223 considers that they might have had "magical import". Undoubtedly, the work is such that we think of extra-sphragistic use easily.

11. Kenna 1969: 31 on the seal-talisman in the Late Bronze Age and, in note 60, declares "In all, there is a significant number to designate a class of seal-talisman but not enough to negate the evidence of the vast majority which are prima facie talismanic."

12. It has been suggested as recently as Yule 1977:69 that gold rings were perhaps the exclusive possession of women (priestesses?). This is contradicted, however, by the gold ring found in Sellopoulo Tomb 4 (Popham and Catling, BSA 1974: 217).

13. The role of women in the Knossos textile industry is stressed in Duhoux 1976: 209-212 though certainly not to the exclusion of men. Women in the wool and textile business of Assur in the Old Assyrian period is vividly brought to life in Veenhof 1972:- the woman Lamassi's extensive correspondence survives to tell of the numerous textiles shipped to Anatolia for which she was paid, through transport contracts, in gold and silver. She ran a home industry, involving all the female members of her household. Besides receiving wool for her own household, she apparently acted as distributor for other households and was paid in silver (Veenhof 1972: 111-118). Another woman speaks of "fifteen textiles of good quality. All this is my production, my goods entrusted for sale with profit", (ibid 110) implying at least a semi-independent status. The existence of a home industry in the houses of the Anatolian merchants cannot be doubted. Obviously, one cannot leap from Assur to Zakro -- even via the o-pi of Knossos -- but one can at least state that the ancient world knew of female industry on a responsible level.

CHAPTER VI

THE INFLUENCE OF THE ZAKRO MASTER

In historical times, it is often not too difficult to trace
the influence of an outstanding artist on his contemporaries or
successors. In prehistory, with so many gaps in the record and
basic chronological problems, tracing one artist's influence
may seem an act of faith. But the strong originality of the
Zakro Master encourages the effort:- copies of his monsters
can hardly pass unnoticed elsewhere and themes which we believe
his may be seen to be adapted by other hands. This is not to
say that anything at all monstrous will be assumed to have been
made under his influence. We have seen an earlier monster
tradition into which others might have dipped independently.
Not all roads of fantasy need lead to Zakro; we shall weigh
probabilities.

Contemporary glyptic material is now fairly broad in its
geographical reach. Besides the sealings from Zakro and Ayia
Triada, we have at least a glimpse into the glyptic art of the
day at Knossos (the Royal Road and, increasingly, the Strati-
graphic Museum excavations) and at Chania where a cache of
sealings was found in the Archives.[1] One would like to make use
only of such excavated material but this would be too limiting
and we too must dip, this time into the pool of purchases,
gifts and chance finds that makes up so much of our collections.

Bucrania

At Zakro itself, there are at least two bucrania which
copy the Zakro Master's work:- Nr 88 and 84. Nr 88 (see MSS
Catalogue of Combinations, Nr 58) seems to be a clear copy of
a lost work by the Zakro Master; the theme is his but the
treatment could not be more different. Head and horns are
schematic, engraving flat. True, the birds are more plump
but they do not emerge organically from the horns (further
discussion of this seal-type in Chapter II). Above the
bucranium float "snake frames" (cf.: Nr 56 and 66) which enclose
a quartered disk, a unique addition.[2] Nr 88 is closely related
to Nr 84, bucranium with loop (MSS Catalogue of Combinations
Nr 30) which may be based on a variant of Nr 80, now lost.
Both sealings suggest a lost original in which a circular object
replaces the double axe or degraded lotus placed above or below
"snake frames".

Just such a seal-type is found at Sklavokampo, SK 17
(Pl. 14 B). It appears on a very damaged nodule; it is
impossible to judge if it represents a copy or, possibly, even
an original by the Zakro Master. A bucranium with stag's horns
(we have already suggested this as an intermediate design
between the Bucranium Series and the Stag's Head Series; see
Chapter III n. 3) has concentric circles (or a rosette) between
its horns; the faintest trace of wings may be seen on either
side of the muzzle.[3] Another bucranium from Sklavokampo, SK 16
(Pl. 14 A right), seems a variant of our Nr 82:- in addition
to the normal complement of horns, downturning, an extra horn
appears, below, which may well have twisted around behind the
head. SK 16 is a variant of Nr 82, not a copy; note the new
wing-like whiskers adorning its cheek. Two more copies -- or
originals -- of the Zakro Master's work are found at Sklavokampo,
the gorgons SK 13 and 14 (our Pl. 14 A left and centre) which
are discussed below.[4] That four Zakro-type sealings were found
at this remote country villa should cause surprise but that
is not the only glyptic tie between the two sites:- the signet
ring impression of a Taurokathapsia, Nr 96, is possibly made
by the same ring as SK 5.[5] Thus, we may postulate some tie
between Zakro and Sklavokampo albeit indirect and via Knossos.[6]

Another copy of a lost work by the Zakro Master may be
seen on a haematite lentoid from the Psychro Cave (?), now in
the Ashmolean Museum (Pl. 13 D). A bucranium with downturned
horns is the focus of the composition; above are two goat
heads in profile, their long horns reaching down to frame the
bucranium. The composition is fully circular. Elongated
goats' horns may be compared with Nr 39 and the opposed protomes
above an animal mask with Nr 56. The gem, however, is not cut
by the Zakro Master:- the engraving is shallow, the surfaces
flat. The individual treatment of the protomes, too, makes
this an adaptation of his work, perhaps a copy -- though not a
slavish one -- of a lost gem.

Fantasy bucrania may also have been made until a rather
late date at Knossos. An example from the Room of the Stone
Bench (Pl. 9 H) continues the separate local tradition seen
earlier in such works as the sealing from the Hieroglyphic
Deposit (Pl. 9 F), and the more naturalistic bucrania
mentioned in Chapter IV n. 5. The Knossos line does not seem
to owe anything to the Zakro Master's influence.

Fantasy Animal Masks

Fantasy Animal Masks other than the Lion Masks of the
talismanic stone do not long survive the Zakro Master. A
possibly contemporary boar's head engraved on one side of a
double-engraved haematite lentoid might be intended as a
naturalistic representation (Pl. 13 G).[7] Large round eyes and
irregular bristles, however, are reminiscent of Nr 67 and 68;
his modest tusks suggest rather a common origin than imitation.
More puzzling is the Boar or Lion Mask on a sealing from Ayia
Triada (Pl. 13 I); its resemblance to the Boar Masks Nr 64 - 66
is clear but it lacks any hint of tusks. The composition, too,
suggests a source other than the Zakro Master. One adaptation
of the Zakro Master's theme seems self-evident:- a steatite
lentoid (Pl. 13 F) shows an animal mask with horns which evolve
into furry small animals, possibly dogs. Its head sprouts a
bristly tuft, similar to the projections on the heads of Nr 69
and 167. Despite my best efforts, no further work from this
most interesting hand was found and, thus, the "furry monster
master" was stillborn.

A direct copy of two of the Zakro Master's seals is seen
on a rare two-sided reel-shaped stone in a private collection
(Pl. 13 C).[8] One side is engraved with a lion's mask (cf.:
Nr 56, 57); the other copies the long-eared owls of Nr 89.
The engraving is said to be rough and the stone's surface flat,
so that there is no doubt that this is not the Master's work.[9]

Gorgons

True gorgons are rare in the Late Bronze Age. Most LBA
examples of frontal human heads are ordinary faces with nothing
of fantasy and nothing frightening added: there is no emphasis
on eyes which makes one doubt that they are meant as apotropaic
beings at all.[10] An exception is the recently excavated lentoid
from a LH IIIA:2 tholos at Nicoria (Pl. 10 I), a gem which would
have been undoubtedly denounced as a forgery were it not from a
scientific excavation.[11] This gorgon has numerous affinities
with those from Zakro:- a triangular face with puffed-out
cheeks (cf.: Nr 44, 45 and, especially, 78); long bristly hair;
perhaps the deep strokes on either side of his head are the
remnants of wings. All such features are part of the common
gorgon fund (Chapter IV) and need not be traced to the Zakro
Master's inspiration (the emphasis on the head alone suggests
another source). Since all other gorgons are LM IB or earlier

and of Cretan or island origin, one suspects that the Nichoria gem is out of its true context, possibly handed down because of proven amuletic efficacy.

A new find from Knossos shows a wingless gorgoneion (Pl. 10 K) painted on an LM IB cup rhyton.[12] Its head is almost round and covered with hair, perhaps implying a beard as well; "streamers" rise upwards from the crown of the head. Its face is further marked to suggest extreme hairiness on an almost bestial level. The mouth is gaping and its eyes wide open and staring. Though contemporary with the Zakro gorgons, the Knossos artist has obviously tapped another source, more in line, perhaps, with such primitive gorgoneions as Pl. 10 A and, especially, the painted Pl. 10 G.

The discovery of the Knossos gorgon head lends credence to a chance find from Ayios Ioannis near Phaestos.[13] This gorgoneion is found on a two-sided lentoid (Pl. 8 C). The obverse is already highly stylized:- obvious gorgon features include obligatory staring eyes and the bristly beard. Its beard (a Bes-like feature?) may be simply a displacement of the usual bristly hair, though the Knossos gorgoneion suggests that this innovation may have already entered the gorgon repertory; in any case, the beard might possibly have survived to influence gorgons of the early archaic age. The reverse of this gem is a further abstraction of the gorgoneion (demonstrating remarkable sophistication) which indicates that both sides were simultaneously engraved. This artist, too, probably owes more to the early abstract gorgons (e.g. Pl. 10 D,F) than to any influence emanating from Zakro.

Two full-figure gorgons appear at Sklavokampo:- SK 13 and 14, found together with two other seal-types on a badly decayed sealing (Pl. 14 A left and centre). Possibly, SK 13 belongs to a Minotaur Series (cf.: Nr 170) rather than the gorgons but SK 14 probably is a true gorgon, not unlike Nr 44 and, especially, Nr 171. Obviously, given its poor state of preservation, it is hazardous in the extreme to venture even the most tentative suggestion that these are works by the Zakro Master but they must be, at least, quite close copies of his work. In any event, the glyptic link between Sklavokampo and Zakro is reinforced.

Bird-Ladies and Bird-Men

Does the honour of inventing the Bird-Lady belong to
the Zakro Master? Our studies have, unfortunately, removed
this palm from his grasp (pages 94 - 95) and it is possible
that even her transformation into a flounced-skirted, spread-
winged dancer was accomplished in an earlier generation:-
the Bird-Lady from Quartier XIII of the Mallia Palace is
assigned by her excavators to a MM III level (Pl. 12 H).[14]
The gem is very worn but the reconstruction of the image
leaves no doubt that a full-fledged Bird-Lady is represented.
Although the ease with which a single stone moves up or down
levels is notorious -- the second, equally worn Mallia Bird-
Lady (Pl. 8 E) was a surface find and useless for dating --
we should not refuse to consider Mallia (NB: Pl. 12 F) as
her home. We must therefore be especially careful when
evaluating the Zakro Master's influence on other Bird-Lady
artists; Mallia might have gone on making an independent
series.[15]

Ayia Triada has four Bird-Ladies in the great sealing
hoard:- AT 102, 103, 104, 105. The Bird-Lady is thus the
only monster (other than griffins) to find favour at this
site. AT 105, in spite of her crude appearance, is used 60
times in the records and must have belonged to a philistine
of some importance (Pl. 14 F). She is a Bird-Lady reduced to
the simplest form; all her feathers have disappeared.
Possibly, AT 105 is related to Zakro Nr 168 (= Levi 1929b:
173, fig. 206), not by the Master's hand. The only suggestion
of his influence may be seen in the bucranium-like body of
the Bird-Lady; it is just possible that he had made an
intermediate type based, for example, on Nr 80. AT 102
(Pl. 14 C), on the other hand, comes close to Zakro 38 in
her pose. Wings are displayed rather than folded back (see
the detailed comparison of the two seal-types in Chapter III
n. 9). One can imagine AT 102 as a copy of a lost Zakro
original, though it need not be, but with the local touch
of an added bench -- the Zakro Master disdains props. Note
the functionless row of bristles along her skirt (cf.: the
wings of Nr 26; the back and chest of Nr 127; possibly a
misunderstanding of the sharply-cut flounces on the folded-
back skirt of Nr 38). That she is at best a copy and not an

original is confirmed by her long, not round breasts, ⌐Nr 38
seems to have an extra row of pear-shaped breasts in addition
to her balancing round one (Pl. 21)⌐, the provision of a
bench, and the static pose.

AT 103 could also be a copy (Pl. 14 D) though a singularly
lifeless one:- her wings are deeply cut and have the characteristic smooth upper wing. But her skirt is heavy and scarcely
drawn from life (cf.: Nr 20, 21); her feet are well drawn but,
since not pigeon-toed, lack all movement. AT 104, though
fragmentary, is more active (Pl. 14 E). She might be a copy,
a slightly more conscientious one, of a Zakro dancing Bird-
Lady; her condition, however, prohibits more than this vague
generalization.

Returning to Zakro, an unpublished Bird-Lady gem was
found in an **apotheke** on the Palace grounds.[16] The lentoid
might have been made at Zakro but not by the Zakro Master.
She is carefully drawn but a bit heavy. Her wings are outstretched; feathers fall from the top. Her aniconic head is
in profile, beak pointing up. The legs seem more bowlegged
than pigeon-toed and, indeed, this Bird-Lady is earthbound.
In front of her skirt, which is not flounced, is a curious
protuberance which I can only liken to a sporran.[17]
This seal, from a LM IB destruction deposit, confirms a
contemporary interest in the Bird-Lady by engravers of
more modest ability.

Another contemporary seal-engraver, or workshop, made an
interesting series of Bird-Ladies and -- the first since the
Protopalatial period -- Bird-Men. The hand is sharply
individual if less inventive than that of the Zakro Master.
I have dubbed this analytical hand the "Royal Road Master"
after the site where one of his gems was excavated.[18] This
is a dark steatite lentoid, HM 1970, (Pl. 26 A) which was found
with LM IB pottery (and rare examples of LM II - III) on the
Royal Road: North at Knossos.[19] The monster is a lion-headed
Bird-Man whose body trails away into a formless tail. The
wings are characteristic, with exaggerated long pinions turning
inwards to form a frame around the body; coarse feathers are
roughly indicated and drop almost, but not quite from the top
of the wings. His lion head, though entirely different from
the animal heads of the Zakro Master, suggests his influence,

111

albeit not at first hand, as do the subsequent, if limited
transformations:-

1. into the Bird-Man (Pl. 26 C) who has the characteristic
   wing of the Royal Road Master as well as a second mark
   of his hand, a long pointed head in profile filled
   with a single, immense eye;

2. into the Bird-Lady in the Metaxas Collection (Pl. 26D)
   from Embaros, whose serrated wings develop from those
   of the preceding type;

3. into the Bird-Lady from Axos, whose entire head has
   become a great eye (Pl. 26B);

4. into the Bird-Lady in the British Museum (Pl. 26 E),
   who has lost her pointed head and sharply flounced
   skirt, but retains the characteristic wings.[20]

These five sealstones are variously dated from LM II - IIIB,
but I suggest that a single workshop is responsible -- best
dated by the bulk of the associated pottery found on the Royal
Road, to LM IB.[21] The first four gems are perhaps the work of a
single analytical individual; the British Museum gem is close
to the group but probably not by the same hand. That three of
the stones have a central Cretan provenance suggests that the
taste for monstrous themes was not just confined to the east.[22]

The Bird-Man's long if intermittent career seems to end
with the rock crystal lentoid from Phigalia (?) in Pl. 11 F,
a demise perhaps hastened by the Zakro Master's indifference.
Here, he seems to drift along the edge of demonology, confused
with the Master of Animals as perhaps the Bird-Lady is muddled
with Potnia Theron on a cylinder seal from Palaikastro (Pl.14G).

Evans was of the opinion that the Bird-Lady type survived
in Crete to the latest Minoan phase and, to my knowledge, this
opinion has not been contradicted.[23] Yet it is curious that
no excavated Bird-Lady comes from a context later than LM IB.[24]
Even the stiff Bird-Lady on a cylinder seal from Palaikastro
(Pl. 14 G) belongs properly to LM IB and not LM II as placed by
her early excavators.[25] Besides the Bird-Ladies of Zakro and
Ayia Triada, there are too few securely dated pieces to allow
of comfortable generalizations (Mallia, Palaikastro, the new
gem from Zakro) but it is at least possible that Bird-Ladies
too are extinct after LM IB (though, of course, some gems could
continue in use long after this period). Put another way, just
because a stone is carelessly made, or the work of a mediocre

artist is not reason enough to relegate it to a later date.
After all, AT 103 and 105, as well as the new gem from Zakro,
were probably made not many years apart from the most exquisite
of the Zakro Master's inventions. Appreciation of a period of
high artistic achievement should include the possibility, if
not the certainty, that this peak was supported by a host of
lesser talents.[26]

Other Winged Monsters

The griffin and the sphinx are undoubtedly the most popular
winged monsters in the Late Bronze Age,yet their evolution owes
little, if anything, to the Zakro Master's elaborate fantasies.[27]

The griffin's stiff crest first appears on Crete in the
Master's work but it is earlier seen on Queen Ah-hotep's axe.
This is assumed to be one of the axe's Aegean features but it
is not impossible that it has a Syrian origin whence it was
picked up and popularized by the Zakro Master.

The diadem worn by the butterfly sphinx, Nr 74, is not the
standard sphinx headdress, a plumed tiara:- the "floating
ornament" is, as we have seen (in Chapter II's discussion of
this seal-type) not part of her tiara but, rather, knobbed
antennae rising from her shoulder. She is thus out of the
evolutionary mainstream which runs, if, as is probable, Evans's
reconstruction is correct, from the ivory sphinx of the East
Treasury deposit at Knossos.[28] The superb butterfly sphinxes
disappear without a trace, a fate, as Evans remarked, their
beauty did not deserve.[29]

Two winged monsters of Ayia Triada, AT 100 and 101 (Pl.
13 H) are found together on a single sealing. AT 100, at
least, is from the hand of the Zakro Master rather than a copy
of his work; AT 101 is too damaged for certainty (See Appendix
I/ 7 - 8). They are thus evidence for official or commercial
relations between the sites, not artistic inter-action.

Two bird-monsters (?) sit and conspire on a quartz a-
mygdaloid in the Heraklion Museum (Pl. 13 E). They might be
related to the more or less naturalistic owls antithetically
disposed on an amygdaloid in the Ashmolean Museum CS K 225.
If so, it shows another route by which monsters might develop
out of the merely odd.

An equally blurred line between natural and fantastic
intentions may be seen on the lovely ivory plaque from LM IB

Palaikastro (Pl. 26 F). Taken by some to be a nature study
of a bird in a rocky landscape,[30] I think rather that we are
seeing an East Cretan artist (from the Zakro Palace ivory
workshop?) under the influence of the Zakro Master.[31] While
the bird's crest might be a conventional depiction of feathers,
his exaggerated fantail is not avian but imaginary. Near at
hand was an artist with such visions and it seems fair to
suggest some interchange of ideas between two craftsmen.[32]

"Snake Frames"

The earliest "snake frames" may be those pictured by the
Zakro Master but, following Della Seta, one is reluctant to
ascribe objects of religious significance to an artist's
imagination.[33] His treatment of the frames, certainly, suggests
no attitude of veneration. While it is true that Nr 66 has a
(half) double-axe above a pair of frames, this is the only hint
of a religious connection. The pair of snake frames, which
becomes orthodox, is rare in his work:- Nr 66 has a pair above
a fox mask and Nr 81 below a bucranium. Otherwise, it is
always but a single "snake frame" growing out of, or transformed
from, tusks.[34]

Something of the same flexibility appears in the (possibly)
earlier Aegina pendant:- a male deity stands in front of a pair
of frames which pass behind him at hip height. The god, holding
two waterbirds by the neck, is a Master of Animals. Compare
the Zakro Master's association of the frames with birds and
animals:- birds grow from the snake frames on Nr 81 (copied by
another artist on Nr 88); frames evolve into small animals on
Nr 60 and 66. The connection between snake frames and wildlife
will endure:- later gems will show the frames with bucrania,
long-horned goats, or, most commonly, the Mistress of Animals
standing between heraldic beasts.[35] The single frame disappears;
double or triple frames are held or float above a bucranium or
the Mistress of Animals. Only once more, on a gold ring from
Dendra (CMS i 215) are the snake frames in a Zakro-like
position:- goats stand within the frames, rather in the manner
of Nr 81, reminding us of horns of consecration.

It is possible that the Zakro Master was living at a time
when the snake frames were coming into religious use.[36] He
seems to have grasped their relationship with birds and animals
but, it must be stressed, hardly held the objects in awe. Only

later, perhaps, was their ritual function fixed and his visions had no part in, nor influence on, their future use.

Knielauf

In Chapter III we discussed how the Zakro Master adapted the oriental Knielauf to indicate swift movement. Since no earlier use of the pose appears in the Aegean, it seems fair to credit him with the importation and transformation of it. What is astonishing is that the pose effectively dies with him. Minoan artists, with their love of movement, did not accept the innovation. Still, it is possible that four gems owe something -- even if only the idea of a monster in Knielauf -- to his influence:- an ass-headed monster conjoined with two dogs disports in the Knielauf on a haematite lentoid from Cyprus (Pl. 15 I); a double-bodied monster kneels rather than runs on a gem from Kato Syme (Pl. 15 F); a Minotaur, possibly double-bodied, almost marries the Knielauf and torsion on a basalt lentoid possibly from Knossos (Pl. 15 H); from the destruction level at Knossos comes a sealing which has a double-bodied monster apparently in the Knielauf. Curiously, the idea is confined to monsters, though not monsters of the Zakro type.[37] Did it, possibly because of its use by the Zakro Master, strike other Minoan artists as essentially a monstrous gait? We can do no more than note the coincidence of its use and the possibly simultaneous disappearance of his monsters and Knielauf.

Perhaps extinction was postponed. Can we cite his influence, however indirect, on two LH IIIB sealings? A sealing from Pylos Palace (Pl. 15 J) shows the Master of Animals in vigorous Knielauf running after griffins and other winged monsters. In a secularized version (?) of the Pylian gem, a hunter in modified Knielauf rushes a lion (Pl. 15 K). Another hunter in Knielauf spears an ibex on an agate lentoid now in the British Museum (CMS vii 131); unfortunately without any provenance, this gem is too flimsy a bridge across the time gap to LH IIIB.[38] Perhaps, rather than postulate re-invention of the Knielauf for swift movement, we may more reasonably ascribe the revival of the pose to recrudescence and not step-by-step continuity.[39] Perhaps, a mainland artist actually saw one of the Zakro Master's gems and was inspired by it -- the only epitaph a prehistoric artist ever has.

CHAPTER VI

1. The iconography of sealings from Zakro, Ayia Triada and
   Chania is compared in Table 1.
2. When any object is inserted into the "snake frames" it
   is almost inevitably a double-axe. On <u>CMS</u> i 379 from the
   Palace of Pylos, a variant with a crown or circle-above-
   crescent appears as the only other exception to the rule.
   Gill 1969: 100-101 has collected and studied "snake frames".
3. This bucranium has the characteristic "V"-shaped brow of
   the Zakro Master's bucrania; cf.: Nr 81 and 87.
4. SK 13, 14 and 16 appear together with a fourth seal-type
   (dancing woman) on an unusual "truncated polyhedron"
   nodule shape. Another combination nodule at Sklavokampo
   pairs two naturalistic seal-types (SK 9 + 10). See
   Marinatos 1948: 90-91.
5. Betts 1967: 24-26 argues that the correspondence of Nr
   96 with SK 5 -- and similar equivalences elsewhere --
   indicates the dependency of both sites to the overlordship
   of Knossos:- "one wonders exactly what the rulers of the
   palaces in the East ... could have found as topics to
   justify direct correspondence with ... the small and
   distant villa at Sklavokampo" (p. 24). He then postulates
   an official from Knossos travelling to various sites with
   the ring (or replica). This is to assume, first, that only
   royalty corresponded (p. 25), a premise which the existence
   of Zakro-type monsters at Sklavokampo (and Ayia Triada)
   calls into question. Secondly, it discounts the arrival of
   two nodules with these type of monsters, in addition to
   the more aristocratic ring, implying some more regular, if
   mundane business. See n. 6 below.
6. Mr Sinclair Hood has kindly pointed out to me that the
   villa of Sklavokampo lies on the route between Lepria --
   the probable major Minoan source for serpentine
   ("steatite") for lapidary use -- and Knossos. See Warren
   1969: 138-139. The raw material for the stone vase maker's
   workshop in the Palace of Zakro, and perhaps for the Zakro
   Master himself, might well be a topic of correspondence
   between the Palace and the distant villa at Sklavokampo.

7. Kenna 1960: 124 dates the boar's head to MM III. Since this dating is based at least in part on his placing the Zakro sealings, with their fantasy animal heads, in his Second Transitional Period, we feel reasonably secure in updating the one now that we have updated the other. The reverse of the lentoid, cow suckling calf, obviously the work of a second hand, could nonetheless be contemporary with the boar's head. See Chapter IV n. 10.

8. Boardman 1970: fig. 80. See Part I, Chapter II n. 14.

9. Boardman 1970: 42 describes the engraving.

10. Xénaki-Sakellariou 1958a: 80-81 lists Neopalatial "gorgons" but omits the one which seems to me most likely to continue the apotropaic tradition:- the frontal-facing goddess, flanked by griffins, who holds up Snake Frames (Hospital Site, Knossos, Warrior Grave III; BSA xlvii 275: III/20).

11. This is Betts's opinion (in his introduction to CMS x, page 23) and it is obviously true.

12. I am most grateful to the Managing Committee of the British School at Athens and to Professor Peter Warren for their permission to publish a reproduction of this cup.

13. That it is a forgery cannot be ruled out (Ingo Pini's opinion in a personal communication). Equally, it has certain clear affinities with gorgons on later Island Gems (cf.: Boardman 1963: 357 and, especially 180). However, the gorgoneion from Knossos allows it to remain, if tentatively, in a LBA context.

14. Chapouthier and Demargne 1942: 9, fig. 46a. Younger 1973: 367, however, places it in a broader MM III-LM I range (on stylistic grounds?) which would leave the question of precedence an open one.

15. If the Bird-Lady was an object of demonolatry, her worship need not have been confined to East Crete. In that case, many more sites might have made independent versions of her image. I would point out, however, the nearly reverse correlation between Bird-Ladies and birds of naturalistic types at Zakro, Ayia Triada and Chania. This suggests that, to some extent, the one replaces the other and that demonology may have had little to do with the choice.

16. Platon 1969: 217.

17. The Zakro gem is similar in some respects to a worn-out Bird-Lady on a double-engraved steatite lentoid (Pl. 7G b).

The bowlegged legs are identical and she too wears a "sporran". Since the Zakro gem is LM IB, surely the other is unlikely to be LM IIIB as given in CMS xii 276.

18. I am grateful to the excavator, Mr Sinclair Hood, for permission to mention and reproduce this gem. Having studied the relevant stones from photographs only, I am naturally hesitant to ascribe various works strictly to the Royal Road Master's own hand. I therefore stretch him into an analytical individual, perhaps a small workshop.

19. Mr Sinclair Hood very kindly communicated to me the pottery associations (letter of 4 February 1981) and the information that V.E.G. Kenna had dated this gem, on stylistic grounds, to LM IIIB.

20. Possibly also by the Royal Road Master are CS K 374 and Giam 373. All stones are of steatite or black marble; all but Giam 373 (a flattened cylinder) are lentoids.

21. The Royal Road gem was dated by Kenna to LM IIIB (see n. 19 above); CMS xii 255 was dated to LM II; CMS iv 290 was dated to LM IIIA:2; CMS vii was dated to LM IIIB.

22. The slightly fantasy bucrania from Knossos (Chapter IV n. 5) may also point to a moderate interest in non-naturalistic subjects. At Ayia Triada, just under 5% of the sealings have fantasy themes, a small but not utterly unimportant group.

23. PM i 708.

24. I simply do not know if CMS v/1 274 from Armeni, Grave 55 (LM IIIA:2 - IIIB) is meant to be a Bird-Lady or not. The editor of the relevant CMS volume, Dr Ingo Pini, prudently describes it as "Wahrscheinlich eine Frauengestalt mit Vogel-kopf und -flügeln"; if it is meant to be a Bird-Lady, it is an entirely different vision of one.

25. Apart from a few sherds there is no LM II at Palaikastro; what the excavators then called LM II is now described as LM IB. Younger 1973: 367 repeats the early classification, leaving her alone in LM II. Kenna 1968: 330 perceptively remarks that this cylinder probably predates LM II "for although the design in many respects is complete and satisfies the requirements of the cylinder seal's trad-itional display of forms ... a certain stiffness still

betrays a sense of unease with the shape of the seal."
Compare the two cylinder seals found in East Crete (PM
iv fig. 434, 435) dated by Evans to LM IA (PM iv 497):-
the bucrania with downturned horns and bristly hair,
fig. 434, are squarely in the East Cretan tradition (see
pages 86 - 87); the dolphins, (cf.: burial jars from
Pachyammos, rhyton from Pseira) may also present an East
Cretan motif presaging the dolphins -- somewhat less
dully arranged -- on the Palaikastro cylinder. The Bird-
Lady on the Palikastro seal is very close to being
confused with the Mistress of Animals (waterfowl, dolphins,
sacred tree).

26. One would have thought, after the discovery of the Mallia
    Stoneworking Atelier, that the straight line continuum of
    glyptic progress would be radically modified, if not
    dropped.

27. Perhaps also derived from the griffin are the occasional
    winged goats:- CMS v 201 from Pyrgos Psilonero on Crete;
    CMS i 316 from the Palace at Pylos; HM 2643 from Trapeza
    Kalou; they are, in any case, quite unrelated to Zakro's
    running winged goatmen.

28. PM iii 415-416, fig. 281.

29. PM i 708.

30. Nilsson 1950: 337 goes so far as to identify it as a
    peacock, claiming that it is the only Minoan bird which
    can be identified with certainty. Presumably, Nilsson
    wished to explain the bird's fantasy tail. The peacock,
    surely, does not arrive from India until the archaic
    age /that this is not a reintroduction is implied by
    the bird's complete absence from mythology/.

31. On the Zakro ivory workshop, see Platon 1966 and BCH
    91 (1967) 772. This is the only known ivory workshop
    outside Knossos.

32. The ivory workshop seems also to have been a stone-
    working atelier and housed a faience factory as well.
    While there is no evidence for gem cutting in the same
    area, fairly close contact between different craftsmen
    is a reasonable supposition; a gem engraver is likely
    to have had contact with a stoneworker at least /at the

Mallia Stoneworking Atelier, it is now clear that only gem engravers worked there; there is no evidence of stone vases or jewellery being made in the same area (O. Pelon in a communication to the Cambridge Colloquium on Minoan Society, 1981). We cannot assume any overlap between the trades at Zakro7.

33. The "snake frames" on the gold pendant of the Aegina Treasure may, of course, be older still:- Higgins 1957: 42 and 1979: 53-54 dates the Treasure between 1700-1550 B.C. and suggests that it originated at Chrysolakkos, Mallia (NB: an eastern site).

34. Gill 1969: 91 notes the apparent development of tusks into "snake frames"and suggests that this transformation is due to some "affinity of form, material or colour." Perhaps the frames were made of horn (ibid. p. 98) though this would not account for the knobs on their ends (ibid. p. 100), there being no evidence for this kind of ornamentation or protection of horns in Minoan Crete. Taking the same point of departure, i.e. the development of tusks into "snake frames", I suggest another solution:- that it is not the tusks which are reminiscent of the frames but the fact of their emergence from the mouths of the animals. If so, I would again point to Bes, the "Serpent-Biter",as the original inspiration for the frames (p. 101) (cf.: Pl. 16 B,D, and 17 C for the "Serpent-Biter in profile):- it is a simple matter to visualize him in frontal view (a rare example, of uncertain date but probably XIX-Dynasty -- see Brunner-Traut 1979: 31-32 -- is our Pl. 18 A) whereupon the snakes would appear as rearing up from either side of his leonine head. It may be that the frames began in such a copy as the Lion Mask with "snake frames", Nr 60 and then migrated more or less logically to the Boar Masks. While this idea returns to the early definition of the "snake frames" as indeed based on snakes, there is no reason to postulate double-headed snakes as, for example Nilsson 1950: 365 - 366, nor to dwell on later elaborations (as ibid. 364) which no longer closely resemble true snakes. If indeed a fairly recent importation into LM I Zakro, the still foreign "snake frames" would allow of artistic innovation rather

than be fixed in form (see Della Seta's remarks on this subject, p. 52 above). The Zakro Master's manipulation of the frames seems to suggest such a flexible moment. Whether he, or others, understood the meaning of Bes as "Serpent-Biter" is doubtful on an island empty of noxious snakes (though the enthusiasm of modern Cretan peasants for the slaughter of innocent snakes -- compare PM iv 183 n. 2 -- should perhaps make one pause).

35. "Snake frames" are collected in Gill 1969.

36. A silver vase, painted in the Temple of Amun at Karnak in Egypt (reign of Thutmosis III), depicts a bucranium with a pair of "snake frames" on which is an ambiguous central object (Gill 1969). Whatever this ambiguous object is, nothing like it appears on Crete which may support the idea of a time of experimentation during which the iconography of the frames remained fluid.

37. The monster with two bodies and but a single head does not appear at Zakro (pace Levi 1929b: 160 who claims that Nr 59 is such a creature). That such monsters were not to the Zakro Master's or local taste is suggested by Nr 128 where the lions each resolutely maintains his own head (cf.: PM iv fig. 577, 578).

38. It is dated by V.E.G. Kenna to LM II on stylistic grounds (CMS vii 131).

39. The idea of recrudescence is borrowed from Benson 1961. Very much the same process may explain those early Island gems (Boardman 1963: 164-65) which copied Bronze Age shapes and, to a more limited degree, motifs.

CONCLUSIONS

HIS PLACE IN PREHISTORY

> Avert the shrieker of the night, the scritch-owl
> from the peoples; away with the bird we may not
> name to the ships that sail so fast. (Festus 314,
> translation J.M. Edmonds in Lyra Graeca III)

The roots of the Zakro Master lie deep in his own East
Cretan country. It has not been too difficult to pinpoint a
source of his inspiration in the ancient tradition of prism
engraving. Similarly, subjects he chose to develop, beyond,
in some cases, all recognition, often were used for centuries
before him. In many ways he was an old-fashioned artist,
content to adapt contemporary naturalism to an earlier
artistic vocabulary:- his figures leap and dance in a most
realistic way, they wear flounced skirts, are goats, have
natural wings, but that is all. They themselves have no place
in the living world. They are as much a part of fantasy as a
gorgon drawn in the first Middle Minoan period.

Even his suggested contact with Egypt or the Syrian coast
smacks of an earlier age. Palace of Minos and Aegyptica are
suggestive of intense artistic interchange in the Middle Minoan
age; this seems to drop off in the early Late Bronze Age to,
perhaps, a one-way street typified by the Theran frescoes and,
a little later, the frescoes of Ayia Triada. At about the
same time, we see how inadequate our conventional archaeological
evidence may be when the Keftiu begin to appear on Egyptian tomb
paintings carrying ingots and elephant tusks such as those
found in the ruins of Zakro Palace.[1] Now, in the first flush
of regular renewed contact with Egypt, ought to be the period
of the Zakro Master's floruit:- in Minoan terms, rather nearer
the beginning of LM IB than its end. There is no reason to
assume that the Zakro Master was still alive when his town was
destroyed. On the contrary, he seems most at home at a time
before strong local traditions began to fade in the light of
the cultural imperialism of Knossos. If this is correct, it
strengthens the case for his seals being used by women. During
his own lifetime. they may have been universally used at Zakro,
and multiple sealings may have been the rule. Within a
generation or so of his death, however, the men of Zakro
switched to the general Minoan custom, adopting naturalistic

sealstones.[2] This may be why his work so utterly dominates the
MSS (Table 5) but is scarce in the SSS. Women are notoriously
conservative in anything touching matters of faith. If they
held on tenaciously to their old stones and habits, it can only
be because the stones were imbued with amuletic powers:- older
ones might be thought the more efficacious. Then, as the stones
wore out, were lost, or even were buried with their owners, they
would be replaced, sometimes by a poor copy, but occasionally,
fashionably, by a "modern" naturalistic gem.

The Zakro Master was certainly outdated by the time of the
LM IB destructions.[3] This is one reason, though not the only
one, why he had so few, if any, followers. Possibly, the Royal
Road Master owes him a debt of inspiration; he was probably
copied by a scant handful of engravers at Ayia Triada and,
possibly, Sklavokampo. Beyond that, the trail peters out.
Even the winged Bird-Lady whose form he fundamentally altered
may not, in fact, have survived him by as much as is usually
supposed. Whether we search for followers of his technique,
innovations, or themes, the result is the same:- slight
contemporary influence, thereafter a blank.

It is difficult to imagine so original an artist having so
little influence on later generations. Is it, indeed, as
recently suggested, that madness was essential to his art, that
the sane could not follow?[4] Was he, literally, inimitable?

Our study of his stylistic development does not suggest
madness. Rather one pictures an unusual imagination but one
capable of experimentation and development and, as such,
controlled. We would probably consider Hieronymus Bosch mad
if we knew nothing whatsoever of later medieval Christian
traditions and had lost the intermediate late Gothic
vocabulary of fantasy and anecdote which he so intensively
expressed.[5] Imagine, too, that Bosch were not a painter but
a seal engraver so that we found his monsters and tormented
visions one by one, rather than as a narrative on canvas.
Insanity must be rejected. It is, in any case, no more than
a screen for our abysmal ignorance of the Zakro Master's
environment and the expressive elements which may have existed
in local arts.

How then can we account for his lack of followers?
Within perhaps a generation of his death, Zakro and all other

provincial centres were destroyed; the palaces were never rebuilt, the towns were long in recovering. One result of the LM IB disasters -- whatever their cause -- was the extinction of local artistic traditions. Vigorous provincial art depends on provincial patronage. Even during the Zakro Master's lifetime, it is likely that patrons began to turn towards Knossos for the latest and best in the arts. Local artists could mimic the capital, making the mediocre natural-istic works which form much of the SSS, or move "down-market", filling poorer or feminine requirements. Not long after, the local patrons vanished entirely.

Those artists who survived the disasters had to move and find new patrons or new outlets for their work. There is some evidence that a gem engraver from Zakro had earlier gone to Mycenae, the Mycenae-Vapheio Lion Master.[6] Had he done so, he would undoubtedly have left his East Cretan boisterousness behind. New patrons at Mycenae, still less at Knossos, would not have cared for the bizarre taste of the east even had our emigrant masters still have had the heart to revive it.

NOTES

CONCLUSIONS: HIS PLACE IN PREHISTORY

1. Platon 1971: 244 interpets the ingots and tusks as
    imports as, ultimately, they indeed must be. There may
    be a richer meaning, however, in their presence in the
    Palace and not in the workshops. Liverani 1979: 93-105
    discusses what he calls the "irrational elements" in
    ancient trade, i.e. the princely exchange of identical
    products. Such prestige trade might explain the Keftiu
    gifts to Pharaoh:- they were once gifts to Minos, some
    of which were stored (at Zakro?) for regal recycling.
2. Our analysis of the Zakro Master's stylistic development
    (Chapter III above) may support such a chronological
    sequence. Briefly, we have postulated three main
    stylistic groupings, presumably in chronological order:-

> Early
>
> Boar Masks
> Lion Masks
> Bucranium Nr 83
> Bird-Ladies, excluding Nr 20, 43, 129
>
> Middle
>
> Leaping Bird-Ladies Nr 20, 43
> Running Winged Figures Nr 34, 35, 36
> Breasted Goat Monster Nr 39
>
> Transitional Link
>
> Squatting Winged Goat Nr 37
>
> Advanced
>
> Bucranium Series Nr 81, 82, 86, 87, 170
> Stag Head Series Nr 92, 92A, 139
> Lion-pawed Bird-Lady Nr 129.

The crucial MSS combinations are:-

> MSS Nr 9 - Nr 164 + 170
> MSS Nr 11 - Nr 98 + 20 + 86
> MSS Nr 19 - Nr 39 + 43
> MSS Nr 31 - Nr 81 + 82 + 108

```
MSS Nr 38 - Nr 12/13 + 87
MSS Nr 42 - Nr  15 + 37 + 54
MSS Nr 59 - Nr 129 + 92
MSS Nr 60 - Nr 129 + 92A
MSS Nr 61 - Nr 129 + 139.
```

All of the middle and advanced types (underlined), with
the exception of the running winged figures, join either
with each other or with naturalistic types. The sample
is small, but it may well be that the latest of the Zakro
Master's work freezes the moment when local Zakro custom,
the MSS, and fantasy seals were yielding to naturalism and,
eventually, the pan-Cretan SSS.

3. Kenna 1960: 50-51 viewed the Zakro Master's "dissolution of
    pure naturalism" as presaging the stiff and formal designs
    of LM II (see page 53 above). I hold, on the contrary,
    that, in everything except his devotion to the lentoid
    shape, the Zakro Master harks back to an earlier age. In
    my view, he is not so much dissolving naturalism as resisting
    its impulse. Even his heraldic scenes -- if they are his --
    are neither stiff nor formal; rather, they are pointedly
    bizarre, often with a witty twist.

4. Gill 1981: 85-86 (see page 54-55 above).

5. Just one example must suffice. In his Garden of Earthly
    Delights, the imagery of the strawberry plant infuses the
    whole painting. Even a general acquaintance with medieval
    allegory would fail to inform us -- had we not the
    testimony of Fra José de Siguenza in 1605 -- that the
    chief characteristic of this fruit is that, once it has
    been eaten, it leaves little taste behind in the mouth
    (cited by J. Rowlands, The Garden of Earthly Delights:
    Hieronymus Bosch. Oxford, 1979: no pagination).

6. Younger 1979: 120 suggests that this Master was a Minoan.
    His early work may have been preserved at Zakro "where,
    therefore, he might have had close connections before he
    moved to Mycenae."

TABLE 1

SEAL-TYPES AT ZAKRO, AYIA TRIADA AND CHANIA*

Seal-Type Iconography	Zakro MSS		Zakro SSS		Ayia Triada		Chania	
	n.	%	n.	%	n.	%	n.	%
Formal								
Geometric/Decorative	7	5.8	6	6.4	4	2.7	—	—
Talismanic/Quasi-talismanic	—	—	2	2.2	7	4.7	2	6.3
Hieroglyphics	—	—	3	3.2	1	.7	—	—
Naturalistic								
Cult scenes	6	5.0	15	16.1	27	18.4	7	21.9
Humans in non-cult scenes	4	3.3	2	2.1	7	4.7	2	6.3
Taurokathapsia	5	4.1	3	3.2	6	4.1	1	3.1
Bovines, non-Taurokathapsia	—	—	5	5.4	13	8.8	3	9.4
Goats, agrimi	—	—	11	11.8	3	2.0	—	—
Other quadrupeds	2	1.7	16	17.2	15	10.2	5	15.6
Dogs	1	.8	2	2.2	4	2.7	2	6.3
Lions, lions attacking prey	7	5.8	6	6.4	19	13.0	2	6.3
Birds, waterfowl	1	.8	—	—	20	13.6	4	12.5
Marine life, butterflies, etc.	—	—	1	1.0	6	4.1	2	6.2

Fantasy

	1	%	2	%	3	%	4	%
Griffins, griffins attacking prey	–	–	7	7.5	6	4.1	1	3.1
Sphinxes	–	–	2	2.2	–	–	–	–
Winged lions, heraldic lions	1	.8	2	2.2	–	–	–	–
Minoan Genius	1	.8	–	–	1	.7	–	–
Bucrania, animal masks	25	20.7	3	3.2	1	.7	1	3.1
Animal or bird protomes	3	2.5	–	–	1	.7	–	–
Other monsters	51	42.1	2	2.2	6	4.1	–	–

Other Subjects

	1	%	2	%	3	%	4	%
Buildings, shrines	3	2.5	–	–	–	–	–	–
Illegible	4	3.3	5	5.4	1	.7	–	–
	121	100%	93	100%	147	100%	32	100%

Summary

	1	%	2	%	3	%	4	%
Formal	7	5.8	11	11.8	12	8.2	2	6.3
Naturalistic	26	21.5	61	65.6	120	81.6	28	87.4
Fantasy	81	66.9	16	17.2	14	9.5	2	6.3
Other Subjects	7	5.8	5	5.4	1	.7	–	–
	121	100%	93	100%	147	100%	32	100%

*Ayia Triada figures compiled from Levi 1929a: 7 – 156; Chania compiled from Pappostolou 1977.

TABLE 2

INVARIABLE COMBINATIONS*

MSS Nr	F[1]	Nr & Shape[2]	Description	Nr & Shape[2]	Description	Nr & Shape[2]	Description
Purely Naturalistic Combinations							
1	37	10S	Cult Procession	97S	Taurokathapsia		
2	7	106E	Scratching dog	186/7–	Cult Procession		
3	6	104L	Minoan Genius	119FC	Coupling goats		
4	6	193FC	Lion tied to pole	227S?	Taurokathapsia		
5	1	3S	Seated Goddess	102S	Taurokathapsia		
6	1	154L*	Lion	190L*	Hunter with spear		
7	1	155L	Lion	237E	Lion		
8	1	192–	Woman with bird	238–	Lion		
Mixed Naturalistic/Fantasy Combinations							
9	1	164–	Displayed bird attacked by lion	170L	Frontal Minotaur		
10	1	142–	Taurokathapsia	46L	Winged Gorgon		

11	1	98E	Taurokathapsia	20L*	Dancing Bird Lady	86L*	Bucranium with wings and cap
12	1	196-	Man saluting (frg)	72L	Rosette butterfly	?	Female skirt

Purely Fantasy Combinations

13	33	71L*	Butterfly sphinx	89L*	Opposed owls & waz
14	19	57L*	Lion Mask & birds	73L*	Opposed axe blades
15	16	36L*	Running winged figure	64L*	Boar Mask with tusks ii
16	15	80L*	Opposed lion sphinx	134L*	Geometric decoration
17	15	23L*	Bird Lady with upraised arms	52L*	Opposed bird protomes
18	12	17L*	Minotaur to right	127L*	Fat hog
19	9	39L*	Breasted Goat Monster	43L*	Leaping Bull-headed Bird-Lady
20	5	18L*	Minotaur to left	83L*	Bucranium & meander
21	3	34L*	Running winged goat	236L*	Asymmetrical Boar Mask
22	2	70L*	Palm Trees	77L*	A tergo sphinx

	1						
23	2	49L*	Opposed dogs & helmet	130L*	Five towers		
24	2	32L*	Bird-Lady in harem skirt	35L*	Goat in skirt		
25	1	27L*	Breasted bird	76L*	Grotesque head		
26	1	40-	Pegasus	50L	Fussy monster		
27	1	55-	Illegible	141-	Boar Mask with wings ii		
28	19	44L*	Gorgon with fantail	48L*	Floral abstraction	78L	Cherub
29	7	25L	Bird-Lady, featureless head & fantail	45L*	Gorgon with fantail head-dress	53L*	Bird protomes on fantail
30	3	58L	Lion Mask with wings	84E	Bucranium with loop	74L	Frontal sphinx
31	2	81L*	Bucranium with wings	82L*	Bucranium with twisted horn	108L	Composite beast
32	2	79L	Monster on haunches	93L	Four lion heads	111-	Back-to-back lions
33	1	38L*	Seated Bird-Lady	167L*	Boar Mask & tusks iv	68L*	Lion Mask with round eyes

*Asterisked numbers indicate that the impressions might be made from a single multifaceted stone.

1. Frequency of Combination. 2. Shape of stone = S (signet), E (elliptical), L (lentoid), FC (flattened cylinder), - (too damaged to suggest recreated outline).

TABLE 3

VARIABLE COMBINATIONS*

MSS Nr	F[1]	Nr & Shape[2]	Description	Nr & Shape[2]	Description	Nr & Shape[2]	Description
Mixed Naturalistic/Fantasy Sets							
34	1	2E	Cult man with staff	62L	Boar Mask with tusks i		
35	1	"	"	26L	Fantasy Bird[3]		
36	2			"	"	66L	Boar Mask & animals
37	1	12/13L	Combat scene[4]	75L	Sphinx in headdress		
38	1	"	"	87L	Bucranium close-up		
39	2	"	"	113L	Lion head		
40	2	"	"	184L	Winged lion		
41	1	"	"	175-	Winged humanoids		
42	1	15L "	Nude man & goats	37L	Squatting winged goat	54L	Opposed eagle griffins
43	1	"	"	59L	Boar Mask & wings	135-	Geometric decoration
44	1	"	"	218-	Squatting Minotaur		

Purely Fantasy Combinations

45	5	24L* Bird Lady with plumed helmet	112L* Gate shrine with lions	60L Lion Mask with Snake Frames
46	2	" "	" "	105S Galloping lions & palms
47	1	51L Opposed lion birds	131- Shields & Shrine	19- Crude Minotaur
48	1	" "	" "	85- Bucranium with legs
49	17	21L* Bird Lady with featureless head	61L* Boar Mask with antennae	28L Bird Lady with fantail head
50	4[5]	" "	" "	29L Bird Lady with fantail head and tail
49A/50A[6]	1	" "	61A- Minor variant 61	28/29?
51	1	22L "Snake Frames"	63L Boar Mask with Snake Frame	56L Lion Mask with Bird Protomes
52	1	" "	"	"
53	3	" "	" "	"
54	4	69L* Double-tusked Lion Mask	67L* Lion Mask with bristly hair	30L Bow-coil
55	1	" "	171- Laid-back Gorgon	?? ?

56	15	90L* Waz-lily	132L* Echina	33L Bird-Lady Gorgon
57	3	"	"	173L Bird-Lady Gorgon with hairy ears
58	30	"	"	88L Bucranium with Snake Frames
59	3	129L Lion-pawed Bird Lady	92L Stag head to left with curved antler	
60	13	"	92A/L Stag head to left w/ straight antler	
61	6	"	139L Stag head to right	

*Asterisked numbers indicate that the impressions might be made from a single multifaceted stone.

1. Frequency of Combination
2. Shape of stone = S (signet), E (elliptical), L (lentoid), FC (flattened cylinder), - (too damaged to suggest recreated outline).
3. This combination is given by Hogarth but Nr 26 is too damaged to ensure it is not a variant.
4. It is fairly certain that Nr 12 and 13, all quite damaged, represent the same combat scene.
5. On several nodules, Nr 29 is indistinguishable from Nr 28 so four examples of Nr 29 is probably a minimum figure. (NB: includes two nodules said to be from Knossos Harbour Town).
6. The crucial Nr 28/29 interchange cannot be confirmed on this very damaged nodule (though one of the two is virtually certain), hence the intermediate MSS Nr.

TABLE 4

THE MSS AND ITS RELATION TO THE ZAKRO MASTER[1,2]

MSS Nr	Frequency	1	2	3	4	5	NC	Illeg.
1	37					10 97		
2	7					106 186/7		
3	6					104 119		
4	6					193 193 227		
5	1					3 102		
6	1					<u>154</u> <u>190</u>		
7	1					155 237		
8	1					192 238		
9	1			170		164		

				170	164	
10	1					
11	1	20		86	98	
12	1	72			196	?
13	33	71	89			
14	19	57		73		
15	16	36	64			
16	15	80		134		
17	15	23	52			
18	12	17	127			
19	9	39	43			
20	5	83	18			
21	3	34	236			
22	2	77	70			

No.						
23	2		49 / 130			
24	2	32 / 35				
25	1	27 / 76				
26	1				50	40 · 55
27	1			141		
28	19	44 / 48	78			
29	7	25 · 45 / 53				
30	3	74 · 58				84
31	2			81 / 82	108	
32	2		79	93 · 111		

33	1		167 68	38
34	1	62		2
35	1			26
36	2	66		26
37	1		75	12/13
38	1		87	12/13
39	2			12/13 113
40	2			12/13 184
41	1	175		12/13
42	1	37 54		15
43	1	59		15 135
44	1		218	15
45	5	24 60	112	
46	2	24	112	105

47	1	51		131	19
48	1	51		131	85
49	17	$\frac{21}{61}$	28		
50	4	$\frac{21}{61}$	29		
51	1	22 63			
52	1	22 56			
53	3	63 56			
54	4	$\frac{69}{67}$	30		
55	1	69 171			?
56	15	$\frac{90}{132}$	33		

57	3	_90_	173		_132_
58	30	_90_		88	_132_
59	3		129		
			92		
60	13		129		
			92A		
61	6		129		
			139		

1. Underlined numbers indicate that the impressions <u>might</u> be made from a single multifaceted stone.

2. 1 = Seal-types attributed to the Zakro Master
   2 = Seal-types probably by the Zakro Master
   3 = Seal-types possibly by the Zakro Master
   4 = Seal-types probably not by the Zakro Master
   5 = Seal-types not by the Zakro Master
   NC = Motifs too simple to classify
   Illeg. = Illegible.

TABLE 5

LENTOIDS ENGRAVED ON BOTH FACES

Nr.	Description	Reference
1.	Steatite, from Little Palace Knossos a) Chanting priest b) Bull's head	PM iv: fig. 167 (our Pl. 7A)
2.	Serpentine, from beside Great Circle Knossos: SEX 79[1] a) Man's head de face b) Woman stooping over stone	Unpublished HM 2807
3.	Serpentine, from house in southeast of site, Knossos: SEX 80[2] a) Woman clasping rock b) Standing deer	Unpublished HM 2815
4.	Amethyst, from Sphoungaras a) Fish, sea urchins, branches b) Two fish	Sphoungaras 45B (our Pl. 7B)
5.	Chalcedony a) Fish and plants b) Rayed star	Giam 119
6.	Sardonyx a) Fish b) Bird?	CMS xii 201
7.	Agate a) Bull struck by lance b) Ewer between sacred horns	CMS vii 65 (our Pl. 7C)
8.	Serpentine a) Agrimi in flying gallop b) Bull struck by lance	CMS viii 47 (our Pl. 7D)
9.	Haematite a) Boar's head with bristles b) Cow suckling calf	CS K 243 (our Pl. 7E)
10.	Carnelian a) Agrimi in trot b) Winged quadruped	AGDS München 70 (our Pl. 7F)

11.	Steatite a) Potnia Theron b) Bird-Lady	CMS xii 276 (our Pl. 7G)
12.	Serpentine, from Fortetsa (?) a) Griffin b) Dancing woman	CMS iv 283 (our Pl. 7H)
13.	Steatite, from Tylissos a) Illegible b) Branches	Et.Crét. iii: 107 fig. 19
14.	Steatite a) Talismanic? b) Geometric design	CMS iv 324
15.	Schist, from Quartier Mu (surface find), Mallia a) Bird-Lady b) Very worn	Et.Crét. xxvi: Nr 258 (our Pl. 8E)
16.	Carnelian a) Talismanic rosette b) Combat scene	CMS v 180 (our Pl. 7J)
17.	Sardonyx a) Deer b) Two men in a ship	CMS vii 65 (our Pl. 8A)
18.	Steatite a) Lion to left b) Lion to left	CS K 30P
19.	Agate a) Two bulls facing b) Lion attacks bull? Frontal human head superimposed	CS K 334 (our Pl. 8B)
20.	Steatite a) Man gesturing b) Lion, very worn	Unpublished HM 140
21.	Material unknown (photograph) a) Frontal human "mask" b) Abstraction of side "a"	HM 2113 (our Pl. 8C)

22.	Jasper (?), from houses north of Palace Knossos	HM 838
	a) Griffin and bull	(our Pl. 8D)
	b) Hawk and hog	
23.	Steatite (?)	HM 2075
	a) Schematic man	
	b) Schematic goats?	
_4	Haematite, near Argive Heraeon	AG Pl. III 18
	a) Couchant boar	
	b) Seated oxen	
25.	Reel-shaped seal, green stone with flat faces[3]	Boardman 1970: fig. 80
	a) Long-eared owls seated head to tail and facing; cf.: Zakro Nr 89	(our Pl. 13C)
	b) Fantasy lion-mask; cf.: Zakro Nr 56, 57	

1. I am most grateful to the excavator, Professor Peter Warren, and the Managing Committee of the British School at Athens for permission to mention these unpublished gems.
2. See n. 1.
3. This seal, in no sense a lentoid, is catalogued here as it is a seal engraved on two faces.

COMPARISON OF SEALINGS FROM ZAKRO AND AYIA TRIADA
WITH SOME REFERENCE TO SEALINGS FROM CHANIA

APPENDIX

COMPARISON OF SEALINGS FROM ZAKRO AND AYIA TRIADA

WITH SOME REFERENCE TO SEALINGS FROM CHANIA

Doro Levi made a detailed comparison of the sealings
from Zakro and Ayia Triada but was primarily concerned with
their various iconographies. He nonetheless remarked several
times on the similar styles of engraving when comparing like
with like:- even at Zakro, he noted, the naturalistic
sealings

> applicato quello stile a piani bassi, levigati e
> sfumati, che abbiamo visto esser proprio di quest'arte
> e di questo periodo a proposito delle impronte di H.
> Triada, mentre per i soggetti mostruosi la mano dell'
> artista si rassegnava a seguire rapidamente i facili
> voli della fantasia, approfondendo lo schema, unico in
> mezzo al campo, con forti luci ed ombre, che precorrono
> quasi lo stile dell'epoca posteriore. (Levi 1929b: 185)

Equally, he noted that those few sealings at Ayia Triada
which had monstrous subjects followed the engraving style
of their counterparts at Zakro:-

> che sono quasi tutte a rilievo molto alto e senza
> secondi piani, come vedremo trattando delle cretule di
> Zakro (Levi 1929a: 148 n. 3)

He concluded that the two deposits were contemporary, placing
them both within the wide limits of MMIII - LMI[1] or, less
precisely but more aesthetically, at the flowering of the
naturalistic style of Minoan art.[2] Since clear stratigraphy
is lacking for the Ayia Triada sealings, it has always seemed
reasonable to date them by the Zakro context, i.e. once LMIA
but now considered LMIB destructions.[3] That both groups of
sealings are contemporary seems undoubted.[4] Therefore, any
important differences between the two should not be of
significant chronological value but may rather reflect
differences of taste, practices or, simply, two schools
of artisans.

First, there are the differences in subject matter which
immediately strike the eye (see Table 1).[5] Yet if we once
again carefully compare like with like, i.e. the Zakro SSS
with the Ayia Triada corpus which is virtually all a single
sealing system, as is that from Chania, the differences fade.
It is only within the Zakro MSS, with its concentration of

A/1

works by the Zakro Master, that we find sharp contrasts in subject matter. Otherwise, cult scenes of all types and naturalistic animal portraits predominate (65.6% of the Zakro SSS, 81.6% at Ayia Triada, and fully 87.4% at Chania), which really testifies to the close artistic and cultural contacts between the major sites of this period. The only important difference in subject matter between the sites (always excluding the MSS) is the frequency of bird and waterfowl studies at Ayia Triada and Chania, a theme entirely absent at Zakro. This may be a matter of local taste or, possibly, evidence of the presence of artists interested in this subject; it is even conceivable that the Zakro Master's Bird-Ladies and other feathered and winged creatures pre-empted the naturalists' approach to the topic at Zakro.

The common character of at least part of the iconography is not matched by similarities in administrative practices, at least not in so far as they can be read from the archaeological record. On the contrary, differences are more striking than similarities. We shall look at four areas where systems seem most to differ.

Foremost among the differences must be reckoned the practice at Ayia Triada and Chania of inscribing sealed nodules with Linear A characters. These characters, which appear on approximately 70% of the nodules at Ayia Triada, but under 20% of those at Chania, are considered, quite reasonably, as some kind of official countermarking system.[6] The practice is virtually unknown at Zakro.[7]

The Multiple Sealing System as we know it from Zakro is extremely rare at Ayia Triada and non-existent at Chania. Of the 1043 nodules studied from Ayia Triada only 16 carried combination sealings, all of them pairs (Table A/1). At Zakro just under 70% of the total nodules studied (360 out of 525) belonged to the MSS. The system is so rare at Ayia Triada that one inevitably wonders if the exceptions represent some sort of foreigners. The combination AT 100 + 101 is very likely to be work from the hand of the Zakro Master (see A/7 below); the combination could therefore indicate either the presence of a man of Zakro or, at least, one who has had close dealings with that Palace. In a second combination are found, curiously enough, two seal-types impressed by rings which have

probably been used at other Cretan sites, AT 110 + 117:-
AT 110 may be found at Sklavokampo and Zakro while AT 117
may be found at Sklavokampo alone.[8] This is certainly
suggestive but the remaining seals are innocuous enough (and
note the presence of four bird studies in this tiny group).[9]
The most that we can say, then, is that the practice of
combination sealings may well be foreign but the seal-owners
need not be.

The frequency with which an individual seal-type is used
also differs markedly. At Ayia Triada, a few individuals seem
to dominate the system:-[10] the owner of seal-type AT 125 (a
cult procession), for example, is responsible for 259 impressions, i.e. 24.8% of all sealings. The top three seal-
owners together made 480 sealings (46.0% of the total). If
we group the next most active -- the next 15 seals which made
more than 10 impressions each -- they account for 833 sealings,
79.9% of all transactions. Zakro seems more egalitarian:- the
top "man" -- a combination must be counted here as a single
user -- made just 37 impressions (7.0% of the total); the top
triumvirate but 100 (19.0%); the next most active eleven
managed only 269 impressions (51.0%). More details are given
in Tables A/2 and A/3, but we may summarize here in tabular
form:-

	Ayia Triada		Zakro	
	Sealings	%	Sealings	%
Top Individual	259	24.8	37	7.0
Top Three Individuals	480	46.0	100	19.0
Next Most Active (+ 10 sealing each)	833	79.9	269	51.0
Least Active (- 10 each)	210	20.1	257	49.0

Even granting the vagaries of preservation and recovery, the
different patterns of seal-use are clear and cannot be due to
pure chance. There is no doubt that, at Ayia Triada, a few
individuals were pre-eminent in the system, whatever it was and
whatever they were, i.e. officials, scribes or private persons.
Simply put, 18 individuals dominated while 114 were "also-rans".
Those 18 apparently worked nearly twice as hard on average as
did the top "people" at Zakro:- they accounted for 48.7
impressions each compared to 26.3 each for the equivalent

A/3

14 leaders at Zakro. The bottom of the pyramid, oddly enough, is not as strongly contrasted:- at Ayia Triada those 114 men who used their seals less than ten times each did only 20.1% of the total work, making an average of 1.8 impressions each; the comparable 141 people at Zakro accomplished 49% of all sealings but their productivity was equal to that of their mates at Ayia Triada, 1.8 impressions each.[11]

Examination of the most intensively used seal-types shows no particular iconography predominating (Tables A/2 and A/3). Rather, all kinds of subjects are used by the leaders (that a cult scene leads at both sites -- and at Chania as well -- is tempting but probably misleading since the next ones down the line seem largely secular). Perhaps more noteworthy is that all three leaders are using probable metal signets, two metal signets in the case of the combination at Zakro (Tables A/4 and A/5). Yet the rest of the probable signet-owners are not outstanding for active participation. There are three times as many signet owners (in percentile terms) at Ayia Triada as at Zakro (19% against only 6%), a fact which may owe more to the persistent popularity of the Zakro Master's lentoids in the upper echelons at Zakro than to any socio-economic distinctions.

A final important difference between the sealing systems at the three sites may be reflected in the different shapes of the nodules themselves. And these, in turn, may reflect different objects sealed. We have already discussed (Part I/ Chapter III above) the various nodules shapes and types found at Zakro. There, we distinguished five shapes with flat bases (Class I - V) and one prismatic form (Class VI). At Ayia Triada, however, with the exception of Class IV and V -- which are the simplest sorts of sealings -- the most common types either do not appear at all at Zakro or appear there in negligible quantities.

One would anticipate finding a good number of Class IV and V nodules at Ayia Triada since they are ostensibly the most appropriate for a single seal impression. Yet Class IV is rare (only 1.5% of all nodules) and Class V not especially common (4.5% of all nodules). All other intact examples had plenty of space for two or even three seal impressions even though almost none had more than one. Thus, it seems fair to say that the sealing shape does not determine the number of seal impressions actually made on the nodule.

The most common shapes at Ayia Triada are prismatic forms, distinct variants of Zakro Class VI (detailed descriptions in Table A/6). There are three such variants, all of which have but a single "string hole" at the top of the nodule rather than at both ends as in Zakro's Class VI:-

- Class VII is piriform in shape, a shape which had already appeared in the Hieroglyphic Deposit at Knossos.[12]
- Class VIII is close in shape to Class VII but the form has become nearly round. It is possible, of course, that this variation is meaningless and due to normal careless-ness or hurry, but it seems better to risk an unnecessary category at the outset of a study in the hope of finding similar shapes elsewhere.
- Class IX is a hybrid geometric form, a "cone pyramid", or a steep-sided cone truncated at the top; its edges can be fairly sharply marked, or roughly indicated; the base is usually quite flat. Unlike other prisms, this class can, and sometime does, have the seal impression on its base rather than its side.

Two entirely new shapes appear at Ayia Triada. First, Class X, a true cone, with single "string hole" at the top and the seal usually, but not always, impressed on its circular base. Then, Class XI, a more or less regular dome shape, the dome itself usually being quite roughly formed so that the seal must be impressed on its smoothed flat bottom; the "string hole", which may be entirely lacking, runs lengthwise through the nodule.

Chania, in its use of nodule shapes, is closer to Ayia Triada than to Zakro, though the issue is not entirely clear-cut. The only prisms to appear at Chania are a very small number of Class VI, the Zakro form, and rather more of Class VII, an Ayia Triada shape,(3.5% and 22.2% of nodules respectively). In its devotion to the use of the simple Class V nodule, however, Chania more resembles Zakro but it has evolved its own variant of Class IV (detailed descriptions in Table A/7).

We have already remarked in Part I, Chapter III that the choice of nodule shape was "neither arbitrary nor individual but followed familiar and often local conventions." (p. 25)

The study of sealings from Ayia Triada and Chania seems to
support this contention:- nodule shapes, in addition to
telling us something of the use to which the sealings may
have been put, also provide a clue to communication and trade
between sites. Linear A countermarks, for example, provide
an obvious administrative link between Ayia Triada and Chania;
this link is reinforced by their shared use of Class VII
nodules. When one discovers nodules, on the other hand, which
are clearly out-of-place where found, for example a "cone-
pyramid" or dome-shape at Zakro, it is reasonable to suspect
a foreign origin (tentatively pointing, in the absence of
contemporary sealings from Knossos, towards Ayia Triada or,
one would not be surprised, Phaestos).[13] Such intermittent
links may again be indicated by the occasional recovery of a
unicum, a nodule shape not elsewhere found; could not the
odd unica represent our first insight into sealing practices
not yet documented, indeed at the missing palatial sites,
perhaps even Knossos?[14]

A NOTE ON THE MONSTERS OF AYIA TRIADA

Ayia Triada's seal owners were not much interested in
monstrous forms:- a mere fourteen seals (out of 147) are
what we would classify as monsters, though it may be doubted
that a person of the time would have regarded as monstrous
such composite beasts as griffins, still less the Minoan
Genius. There are six griffin seals (AT 94-99), a signet
ring with a Minoan Genius (AT 107), and a small cynocephalus
ape (AT 106) who may be compared with Zakro Nr 5. Four Bird-
Ladies are found (AT 102-105), none by the hand of the Zakro
Master, though the pose of AT 103 might be an indirect copy
of Zakro Nr 38 (see pages 110-111 above).
Among the rare combination sealings at Ayia Triada, on
a Class II nodule, is the combination (twice) AT 100 + 101,
a Lion-headed Bird + Opposed Lion-sphinx. Both monsters are
almost certainly from the hand of the Zakro Master (Pl. 13 H):-

AT 100 Lion-headed Bird. The monster's features, the
cast of the head, and even the collar, are identical with
those of Zakro Nr 51. The Ayia Triada monster has exchanged
the arms of Nr 51 for wings of canonical type. Such inter-
changeability of wings and arms is seen frequently in the
Bird-Lady series and once in the Bucranium series (cf.: Nr 86
and 170).
Conclusion: Yes

AT 101 Opposed Lion-sphinx. A very damaged image but
apparently a variant of Zakro Nr 80 and 175, both opposed
lion-sphinxes. Given the rarity of the subject, one may
reasonably conclude that this example too is by the hand
of the Zakro Master. Its very poor condition, however, makes
us hesitate, and we must be content with an analytical
individual.
Conclusion: Probably

Although there are so few monstrous types at Ayia Triada,
they are among the most commonly used seal-types. The opposed
griffins of AT 95 is used 102 times (the third most common
seal-type); the crude Bird-Lady, AT 105, is found 60 times
(proof, perhaps, that artistic ability is not a prerequisite

A/7

for commercial or official success); another griffin, AT 99,
is used 24 times and the little cynocephalus ape, AT 106,
twenty times.

APPENDIX

1. Levi 1929b: 185
2. Levi 1929a: 146.
3. Discussion of Zakro dating, see pages 3 - 4 above. The Archive at Chania is also an LMIB destruction; see Papapostolou 1977: 24.
4. Nonetheless, Kenna 1960:50 points out that Ayia Triada has more seal shapes common to Middle Minoan and the so-called Second Transitional Period, while Zakro favours shapes more current in early Late Minoan. This, of course, is at least partly due to the Zakro Master's exclusive use of lentoids. Had Kenna considered subject matter rather than solely shapes, he might have concluded the opposite:- for example, more Hieroglyphic seals at Zakro and more Talismanic seals (used for sealing!) at Ayia Triada.
5. See Levi 1929b: 185 - 201, and Kenna 1960: 49 - 50.
6. Levi 1929a: 73 - 85; Pope 1960.
7. Two exceptions to the Zakro rule are discussed in J. Weingarten, "Two Inscribed Sealings from Zakro", Kadmos 1983 (forthcoming).
8. Betts 1967: 16 - 18.
9. The only Ayia Triada triplet combination, AT 20 + 47 + 112, occurs on a small prismatic bar, apparently a local innovation.
10. Ayia Triada percentages are here based on a total of 1043 nodules which I examined in the Heraklion Museum, and not the 1165 given by Levi 1929a: 73.
11. The comparable figures from Chania, which, being so few must be viewed with considerable caution, are:-

	Sealings	%
Top Individual	25	32.0
Top Three Individuals	42	54.0%
Least Active (- 10 each)	36	46.0%

   Six seals could not be identified due to damage.
12. Heraklion Museum number unknown (= PM i fig. 504d).
13. The out-of-place foreigners will be the subject of a forthcoming article.

14. AT 82, a scratching dog, for example is found on such a
    <u>unicum</u> (Levi 1929a: 110 lists two impressions of AT 82 but
    I could find only this one) : a distinct gable-shaped
    nodule not, to my knowledge, found elsewhere. This nodule,
    which carries a unique inscription as well, will be the
    subject of a forthcoming note.

AYIA TRIADA COMBINATION SEALINGS[1]

Frequency	AT Nr & Shape	Nodule Class	Description
4	39S	II	Lion to right
	133S		Long-necked fantasy animals
2	100L[2]	II	Lion-Bird monster
	101L		Opposed Lion-sphinx
1	40E[3]	II	Lion to left
	24L		Four Swans
1	40E	II	Lion to left
	58L		Bulls couchant
1	143S	II	Descending goddess
	114S		Combat scene
1	143S	II	Descending goddess
	144L		Human & animal
1	7L	II	Opposed bucrania
	42L		Lion to left
1	22L	IV	Two waterbirds
	92L		Small animals
1	26L	II	Three waterbirds
	87L		Lion attacking bull
1	28L	IV	Flying eagle
	141S		Cult scene
1	110S[4]	IV	Charging bull
	117S		Charioteer
1	62L	IV	Bull (frg.)
	126L		Man in cult dress

NOTES

1. None of the combination nodules are inscribed. One
    combination -- a unique triplet -- occurs on a prismatic
    bar and is inscribed with the oil and corn ideograms and
    the number "3".
2. Both seals are by the Zakro Master's hand; see page A/7.
3. AT 40 perhaps appears once more by itself on an inscribed

A/11

clay disk (Pope 1960: 208).

4. Sealings impressed by the same (?) ring as AT 110 are
    found at Sklavokampo (Marinatos 1948: 89-90; Nr 625)
    and at Zakro (Hogarth 1902b: 86; Nr 97). Sealings
    impressed by the same (?) ring as AT 117 are found at
    Sklavokampo (Marinatos 1948: 90; Nr 632-635). See
    Betts 1967: 18.

AYIA TRIADA MOST FREQUENT SEAL-TYPES

(compiled from Levi 1929a and Pope 1960)

Frequency	AT Nr & Shape	Description
251	125S	Cult procession
123	13FC	Flying bird
102	95L	Griffins
60	105L	Crude Bird-Lady
45	118E[1]	Goddess in boat
42	79E	Gazelles
38	19L	Waterbird
38	31L	Insect
28	9L	Talismanic design
25	45L	Lion
24	99L	Female griffin
20	106L	Cynocephalic ape
17	116L	Figure-of-eight shield
14	34L	Argonauts
13	68L	Quadruped
13	32L	Dolphins
12	12L	Geometric design
12	33L	Fish
8	119L	Woman in cult dress
6	122E	Women in cult dance
5	38L	Lioness
5	123L	Woman carrying cult paraphernalia
5	140S	Women and sacred tree
5	2FC	Hieroglyphics
5	25L	Flying swans
5	135S	Cult procession with double axe

NOTES

1. All examples of AT 118 were found together in a storeroom
   to the south of the Northwest area of the Palace (where
   all other sealings were found). Note that none of them
   bear any marks of sealing attachment or string holes so
   one may doubt that they are true sealings at all; all are
   of Class XI (dome) nodule shape.

ZAKRO MOST FREQUENTLY USED SEALS

Frequency[1]	MSS/SS Nr.	Seal-Type(s)
37	1	97 + 10
33	13	71 + 89
30	58	88 + 90 + 132
19	14	57 + 73
19	28	44 + 48 + 78
17	49	21 + 61 + 28
16	15	36 + 64
15	16	80 + 134
15	17	23 + 52
15	56	33 + 90 + 132
13	60	129 + 92A
12	18	17 + 127

- -

16		16
12		8

NOTES

1. In the MSS we are counting the number of times each
   <u>combination</u> appears. Those seal-types which occur in
   Variable Combinations will naturally have a higher total
   if all if their appearances are counted together. Thus,
   Nr 90 + 132 appear 48 times (MSS Nr 56 - 58) for example.

PROBABLE METAL SIGNETS[1] AT AYIA TRIADA AND THEIR USES

Frequency	Nr	Description	+	Description
251	125	Cult procession		
42	79	Gazelles in gallop		
5	25	Flying swans		
5	135	Hide-clad figures & dancer		
5	140	Cult scene with women		
1	114	Combat scene	143S	Goddess scene
4	132	Woman & Babylonian dragon		
4	39	Lion	133S	Fantasy animals
3	54	Taurokathapsia		
3	110	Charging bull[2]	117S	Charioteer[2]
2	143	Goddess scene	144L	Human & beast
1	23	Three waterbirds		
1	51	Bull in flying gallop		
1	80	Wild boar		
1	85	Two dogs		
1	107	Minoan Genius		
1	113	Combat scene		
1	124	Cult procession		
1	129	Woman & goat		
1	137	Women dancing by tree		
1	138	Cult scene with women		
1	139	Woman, rocks, trees		
1	141	Cult scene	28L	Flying eagle
1	145	Taurokathapsia		
1	146	Lions gallop past palms[2]		

NOTES

1. The difficulty of determining the shape of the impressing agent of often damaged impressions needs no emphasis. Levi 1929a notes the signets AT 23, 39, 51, 54, 107, 80, 85, 132, 133, 137, 141, 143; Kenna 1960 suggests AT 25, 110, 113, 114, 124, 125, 129, 135, 137-140, 143. That two such scholars agree on but two impressions (AT 137 & 143) is sobering. Yule 1977 lists a total of 39 rings which seems over-generous·(I compromise with 28 as probable).

2. For this ring at other sites (?) see Betts 1967: 16 - 18.

PROBABLE METAL SIGNETS[1] AT ZAKRO AND THEIR USES

Frequency	Nr	Description	+	Description
37	10	Cult procession	97S	Taurokathapsia
2	1	Descending goddess		
2	105	Lions gallop past palms[2]	24L	Bird-Lady +
			112L	Gate shrine
1	3	Seated Goddess[3]	102S	Taurokathapsia
1	6	Cult procession		
1	11	Cult scene? 3 figures		
1	96	Taurokathapsia[2]		
1	183	Griffin attacks lion		
1	189	Taurokathapsia		
1	195	Cult scene		

NOTES

1. See remarks in A/Table 4 n. 1. Hogarth offered no opinion on impressions made by signets. Levi 1929b mentions just two signets in his additional remarks, Nr 183 and 195. Kenna 1960 allows only two in all, Nr 10 and 11. Yule 1977 seems again over-generous with 26 rings; I compromise with less than half that number.
2. For this ring at other sites (?) see Betts 1967: 16 - 18.
3. Possibly made by a ring fabricated at the same time as, if not from the same ring as, the famous clay "matrix" from the Room of the Egyptian Beans at Knossos (from a level "no later than LMI"; PM i 767 - 770) and the many sealings in the East-West Corridor of the Domestic Deposit (destruction level).

TYPOLOGICAL INVENTORY OF SEALING SHAPES AT AYIA TRIADA

    New shapes at Ayia Triada (for Zakro shapes see above, Part I, Chapter III):-

Class VII

Modified triangular prism with "string hole" only at the top of the nodule, the bottom being closed. The base spreads out to make a piriform shape.

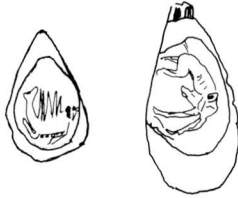

Class VIII

A variant of Class VII, becoming almost round.

Class IX

"Cone-pyramid" or steep-sided cone with truncated top. The edges may be clearly marked or roughly indicated. The base is usually fairly flat. The seal impression is usually on the side, as with other prisms, but may be on the base instead.

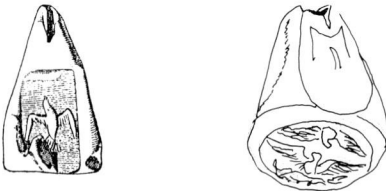

Class X

A true conical shape with a single "string hole" at the top;
the seal is usually impressed on the flat circular base but,
occasionally, is made on the slope of the cone instead. Size
of the cone varies but some examples are extremely tiny.

Class XI

Dome shape, with or without "string hole" (if with, the hole
runs lengthwise through the nodule). The dome itself is often
quite irregular and rough while the base is smoothed to take
the seal impression.

(A/19)

CHARACTERISTIC SEALING SHAPES AT AYIA TRIADA

| | | | | | Frequency in each Class | | | | | | |
Seal-Type	II	IV	V	VI	VII	VIII	IX	X	XI	Other	NC[1]
125		1		12	244	2					
13						2	122				
95			1	3	22	1	60	10			
105				4	52	4					
19				7	33			1			
118									41		
79					37						
45					19	5		1			
99					18	4					
9					5	1	21				
106					7	6			7		
116	1				1	1	10	3			
?					12	3					
32								13			
12			1		2	8			1		
33					7	3		2			
34					6	1		5			
119					5	2	1				

(A/20)									
122						6			
2						6			
123				3	2	3			
135							5		
17						2			
25						4			
18				4		4			
38									
8				4	1	3			
43		1		4					
3									
39 + 133				3					4
136									
54				1		2	3		
63									
78			3				2		
59								1	
151?									
140						3	1		
74	3			3		1			
65				2					
73				2					

(A/21)

68					2							
70		2			1							
114		1			1			1				
76		2										
60												
93								2				
114 + 143	1											
100 + 101	2											
102							1	1				
103								1				
129			2									
110 + 117		1					1			1		
104						2						
15						2						
6						1						
14											2	
10								1				
52		1					1					1
117												1
40		1										
40 + 24				1								

(A/22)

40 + 58	1			2			
48			2				
27							
41	1		1		1		
7 + 42		1					
22 + 92	1		1				
26 + 87							
28 + 141		1					
62 + 126		1				1	
143 + 144	1		1				
1			1		3		1
4							
5							
11			1	1		1	
16							
21				1			
23			1	1			
29			1				
30							
35			1		3		
36							
37							

(A/23)
41
46
49
51
53
55
56
57
61
64
66
67
69
71
77
78
80
81
82
85
86
88

(A/24)

89
90
91
94
96
97
98
108
112
113
120
121
115
124
127
128
130
131
134
137
138
139

(A/25)

	II	IV	V	VI	VII	VIII	IX	X	XI	Other	NC
140					1						
142					1						
150			1								
152					1						
158							1				
153											1
155											1
??		1	1		1		1				
Total											
Nodules	13	16	47	27	524	53	250	49	56	2	6
%	1.2%	1.5%	4.5%	2.6%	50.2%	5.1%	24.0%	4.7%	5.4%	.2%	.6%

NOTES

1. Nodules too damaged to classify by shape.

SUMMARY OF SEALING SHAPES AT CHANIA

The characteristic shapes used at Chania are V, VI, VII, and a local variant of IV. Class IV is perhaps more a modified V than a true variant -- sides are less steep and the profile less triangular than in the normal Class IV -- but, as there is just possibly place for a second impression, though this is never used, a separate category seems indicated.

Seal-type				Frequency in each Class							
II	IVα	V	VI	VII	VIII	IX	X	XI	Other	NC[1]
Nodules		11	44	3	19				2		7
%		12.8%	51.1%	3.5%	22.1%				2.4%		8.1%

NOTES

1. Nodules too damaged to classify by shape.

BIBLIOGRAPHY

In addition to the standard abbreviations (following
AJA 82/1), the following have been used:-

AGDS   Antike Gemmen in deutschen Sammlungen. München
                1968 -   .

CMS   Corpus der Minoischen und Mykenischen Siegel.
                Berlin 1964 -   .

CS K   Cretan Seals (= Kenna 1960) Kenna catalogue number.

Giam   Les Cachets minoens de la Collection Giamalakis
                (= Xénaki-Sakellariou 1958a).

K-MG   Die Kretisch-Mykenische Glyptik und ihre gegen-
                wärtigen Probleme (ed. F. Matz) (Deutsche
                Forschungsgemeinschaft). Bonn 1974.

P2KS   Pepragmena tou B' Diethnous Kretologikou Synedriou.
                Athens 1968.

P3KS   Pepragmena tou C' Diethnous Kretologikou Synedriou.
                Athens 1973.

PM   The Palace of Minos at Knossos (= Evans 1921-1935).

Alp, S.
    1968   Zylinder- und Stempel-Siegel aus Karahöyük bei
             Konya. Ankara.
Altenmüller, H.
    1964   Die Apotropaia und die Götter Mittelägyptens.
             Doctoral dissertation. München.
Ballod, F.
    1913   Prolegomena zur Geschichte der Zwerghaften Götter
             in Ägypten. Moscow.

Benson, J.L.

1961   A Problem in Cretan Orientalizing Birds. <u>JNES</u> 20

        73 - 84.

Betancourt, P.P.

1973   The Polyps Workshop: A Stylistic Group from LMIB.

        <u>AJA</u> 77: 333 - 35.

Betts, J.H.

1967   New Light on Minoan Bureaucracy. <u>Kadmos</u> 6: 15-40.

1976   Late Minoan-Mycenaean Gem Workshops. <u>BICS</u> 23:

        122 - 23.

Biesantz, H.

1954   <u>Kretisch-Mykenische Siegelbilder</u>. Marburg.

Bisi, A.M.

1965   <u>Il Grifone</u>: <u>Storia di un motivo iconographico</u>

        <u>nell'antico Oriente mediterraneo</u>. Roma.

Boardman, J.

1961   <u>The Cretan Collection in Oxford</u>: <u>The Dictaean Cave</u>

        <u>and Iron Age Crete</u>. Oxford.

1963   <u>Island Gems</u>. London.

1970   <u>Greek Gems and Finger Rings</u>. London.

Brice, W.C. & Platon, N.

1975   <u>Inscribed Tablets and Pithos of Linear A System from</u>

        <u>Zakro</u>. Athens.

Brunner-Traut, E.

1970   Gravidenflasche: Das Salben des Mutterleibes. In

        <u>Archäologie und Altes Testament</u>: <u>Festschrift für</u>

        <u>K</u>. <u>Galling</u> (eds. A. Kuschke & E. Kutsch) 35 - 48.

        Tübingen.

1979   <u>Egyptian Artists' Sketches</u>: <u>Figured Ostraka from the</u>

        <u>Gayer-Anderson Collection in the Fitzwilliam Museum</u>,

        <u>Cambridge</u>. Cambridge.

Brunton, G. & Engelbach, R.

1927   Gurob (BSAE 41). London.

Buchanan, B.

1966   Catalogue of Ancient Near Eastern Seals in the
        Ashmolean Museum. Oxford.

Chadwick, J.

1976   The Mycenaean World. Cambridge.

Chapouthier, F.

1932   A travers trois gemmes prismatiques. In Mélanges
        Glotz I: 184 - 201. Paris.

1946   La Glyptique crétoise et continuité de la
        civilization minoenne. BCH 70: 78 - 90.

1951   Le Prisme triangulaire dans la glyptique minoenne.
        BSA 46: 42 - 44.

Chapouthier, F. & Demargne, P.

1942   Fouilles Exécutées à Mallia, Troisième Rapport:
        Exploration du Palais (1927-1932) (Études Crétoises
        vi). Paris.

Collon, D.

1975   The Seal Impressions from Tell Atchana/Alalakh.
        Neukirchen-Vluyn.

Contenau, G.

1922   La Glyptique Syro-Hittite. Paris.

1926   Les tablettes de Kerkouk et les origines de la
        civilisation assyrienne. Paris.

Davis, T,M., Maspero, G. & Newberry, P.E.

1907   The Tomb of Iouiya and Touiyou. London.

Dawkins, R.S.

1903   Pottery from Zakro. JHS 23: 248 - 60.

1905   Excavations at Palaikastro iv. BSA xi: 258 - 92.

Decamps de Mertzenfeld, C.

1938   Les Ivoires de Megiddo. Syria 19: 345 - 54.

Della Seta, A.

1914   Religion and Art: A Study in the Evolution of
        Sculpture, Painting and Architecture. London..

Demargne, P.

1932   Deux Représentations de la Déesse minoenne. In
        Mélanges Glotz I: 305 - 14. Paris.

Dessenne, A.

1951   Le Sphinx: étude iconographique I: Des origines à
        la fin du second millénaire (Bibliothèque des Écoles
        françaises d'Athènes et de Rome). Paris.

1957a   Le Griffon créto-mycénien: inventaire et remarques.
        BCH 81: 203 - 15.

1957b   Les Ateliers de Pierre Gravées à Mallia. CRAI
        123 - 28.

Detournay, B., Poursat, J.-C. & Vandenabeele, F.

1980   Fouilles éxecutées à Mallia: Quartier Mu II (Études
        Crétoises xxvi). Paris.

Duhoux, Y.

1976   Aspects du Vocabulaire Économique Mycénien.
        Amsterdam.

Eals, N.R.

1973   Griffins in Post-Minoan Cretan Art. Doctoral
        dissertation, University of Missouri.

van Effenterre, H.

1973   A propos de l'usage des sceaux dans l'administration
        crétoise à l'époque minoenne. P3KS 361 - 68.

van Effenterre, H. & M.

1974   Vers une grammaire de la glyptique créto-mycénienne.
        K-MG 22 - 29.

Evans, A.J.

    1921-   The Palace of Minos at Knossos (4 volumes in 6).

    1935   London.

Focillon, H.

    1970   Vie des Formes. Paris.

Furtwängler, A.

    1900   Die Antiken Gemmen:Geschichte de Steinschneidekunst

            in Klassischen Altertum. Leipzig & Berlin.

Furumark, A.

    1950   The Settlement at Ialysos and Aegean History, c.

            1550 - 1400 B.C. OpusArch 6: 150 - 271.

    1972   Mycenaean Pottery II: Chronology. Stockholm.

Gill, M.A.V.

    1964   The Minoan Genius. AthMitt 79: 1 - 21.

    1965   The Knossos Sealings: Provenance and Identification.

            BSA 60: 58 - 98.

    1969   The Minoan "Frame" on an Egyptian Relief. Kadmos

            8: 85 - 102.

    1981   The Human Element in Minoan and Mycenaean Glyptic.

            In CMS Beiheft I: Studien zur minoischen und

            helladischen Glyptik: 83 - 90. Berlin

Hazzidakis, J.

    1921   Tylissos à l'époque minoenne. Paris.

Higgins, R.

    1957   The Aegina Treasure Reconsidered. BSA 52: 42 - 57.

    1979   The Aegina Treasure: An Archaeological Mystery.

            London.

Hogarth, D.G.

    1901   Excavations at Zakro, Crete. BSA 7: 121 - 49.

    1902a   Bronze-Age Vases from Zakro. JHS 22: 333 - 38.

    1902b   The Zakro Sealings. BSA 17: 76 - 93.

1911   Note on Two Zakro Sealings. <u>BSA</u> 17: 264 - 65.

Hood, S.

1971   The <u>Minoans</u>: <u>Crete</u> <u>in</u> <u>the</u> <u>Bronze</u> <u>Age</u>. London.

1978   The <u>Arts</u> <u>in</u> <u>Prehistoric</u> <u>Greece</u>. Harmondsworth.

Hutchinson, R.W.

1962   <u>Prehistoric</u> <u>Crete</u>. Harmondsworth.

Huxley, G.L.

1972   <u>Minoans</u> <u>in</u> <u>Greek</u> <u>Sources</u>. Belfast.

Isaac, D.

1938   Les démons minoens. <u>RHR</u> 118: 55 - 91

Kantor, H.

1962   A Bronze Plaque with Relief Decoration from Tell
         Tainat. <u>JNES</u> 21: 93 - 117.

Kempinski, A. & Avi-Yonah, M.

1979   <u>Syrien-Palästina</u> <u>II</u>: <u>Von</u> <u>der</u> <u>mittleren</u> <u>Bronzezeit</u>
         <u>bis</u> <u>zum</u> <u>Ende</u> <u>der</u> <u>Klassik</u>, <u>2200</u> <u>v</u>. <u>Chr</u>.- <u>324</u> <u>n</u>. <u>Chr</u>.
         München.

Kenna, V.E.G.

1960   <u>Cretan</u> <u>Seals</u> <u>with</u> <u>a</u> <u>Catalogue</u> <u>of</u> <u>the</u> <u>Minoan</u> <u>Gems</u> <u>in</u>
         <u>the</u> <u>Ashmolean</u> <u>Museum</u>. Oxford.

1964   The Historical Implications of Cretan Seals. <u>AA</u>
         911 - 54.

1968   Crete and the Use of the Cylinder Seal. <u>AJA</u> 72:
         321 - 36.

1969   The <u>Cretan</u> <u>Talismanic</u> <u>Seal</u> <u>in</u> <u>the</u> <u>Late</u> <u>Bronze</u> <u>Age</u>.
         SIMA 24. Lund.

Killen, J.T.

1967   The Knossos <u>o-pi</u> Tablets. <u>Atti</u> <u>e</u> <u>memorie</u> <u>del</u> <u>1</u>[o]
         <u>Congresso</u> <u>internazionale</u> <u>di</u> <u>micenologia</u>: 636 -
         43. Roma.

Laviosa, C.

1969   La Collezione di sigilli e cretule minoico-micenei
del Museo Archeologico di Firenze. SMEA 10
(Incunabola Graceca 40): 7 - 18.

Levi, D.

1929a   Le Cretule di Haghia Triada. ASAtene 8-9 (1925 -
1926): 7 - 156.

1929b   Le Cretule di Zakro. ASAtene 8-9 (1925-1926) 157 -
201.

1976   Festòs e la Civiltà' Minoica. Roma.

Liverni, M.

1979   Three Amarna Essays. (Sources and Monographs on the
Ancient Near East 1/5). Malibu, California.

Marinatos, S.

1948   To Minoikon megaron Sklavokampou. ArchEph 1939 -
1940: 69 - 96.

1951   Some General Notes on the Minoan Written Documents.
Minos I: 39 - 42.

1966   Polydipsion Argos. In Proceedings of the Cambridge
Colloquium on Mycenaean Studies (eds. L. Palmer &
J. Chadwick) 265 - 74. Cambridge.

Matz, Fr.

1928   Die Frühkretischen Siegel. Leipzig & Berlin.

Mogensen, M.

1930   La Glyptothèque Ny Carlsberg. Copenhagen.

Mountjoy, P.A.

1977   Attributions in the LMIB Marine Style. AJA 81:
557 - 60.

Muller, J.

1979   Individual Variation in Art Styles. In The
Individual in Prehistory: Studies in Variability

in Style in Prehistoric Technologies (eds. J.N.
Hill & J. Gunn) 23 - 39. New York, San Francisco,
London.

Murray, M.A.

1911   Figure Vases in Egypt. BSAE Historical Studies II:
40 - 46. London.

Naville, E.

1900   The Temple of Deir el Bahari (EEF). London.

Nilsson, M.P.

1950   The Minoan-Mycenaean Religion and its Survival in
Greek Religion (2nd ed.). Lund.

von der Osten, H.

1967   Altorientalische Siegelsteine der Sammlung Hans
Silvius von Aulock. (Studia Ethnographica Upsaliensia
xiii). Uppsala.

Padró i Parcerisa, J.

1978   El Déu Bes: Introducció al seu estudi. Fonaments
Prehistòria i Món Antic als Països Catalans I:
19 - 41.

Papapostolou, I.A.

1977   Ta Sphragismata tou Chaniou. Athens.

Pendlebury, J.D.S.

1930   Aegyptiaca: A Catalogue of Egyptian Objects in the
Aegean Area. Cambridge.

1939   The Archaeology of Crete: An Introduction. London.

Petrie, W.M. Flinders

1890   Kahun, Gurob and Hawara. London.

1891   Illahun, Kahun, Gurob. London.

1900   Dendereh. London.

Pini, I.

1983   Neue Beobachtungen zu den Tönernen Siegelabdrücken
von Zakro. _AA_ 1983 heft 4 (forthcoming).

Platon, N.

1969   Anaskaphe Zakrou. _Praktika_ 197 - 237.

1971   _Zakros: The Discovery of a Lost Palace of Ancient
Crete_. New York.

1979   Zakros. _Ergon_: 33 - 35.

Pope, M.

1960   _Cretulae_ and the Linear A Accounting System. _BSA_
55: 200 - 10.

Popham, M.R.

1967   late Minoan Pottery, A Summary. _BSA_ 62: 337 - 51.

Porada, E.

1957   Syrian Seal Impressions on Tablets Dated in the Time
of Hammurabi and Samsu-Iluna. _JNES_ 16: 192 - 97.

Poursat, J.C.

1973   Le Sphinx minoen: un nouveau document. In _Antichità
Cretesi: studi in onore di Doro Levi I_ (eds. G.P.
Carratelli & G. Rizza) 111 - 114. Catania.

Sakellarakis, Y. & Sapouna-Sakellarakis, E.

1981   Drama of Death in a Minoan Temple. _National
Geographic_ cliv (February): 204 - 223.

Säve-Söderbergh, T.

1957   _Four XVIII Dynasty Tombs_. Oxford.

Schiering, W.

1974   Formale Gesichtspunkte zu einigen Motiven auf den
sog. Talismanic Stones. _K-MG_ 143 - 148.

Schneider, H.D. (ed.)

1981   _Rijksmuseum van Oudheden, Leiden_. Leiden.

Seyrig, H.

    1955   Antiquitiés syriennes 60: quelques cylindres
            orientaux. _Syria_ 32: 29 - 43.

Smith, W.S.

    1965   _Art and Architecture of Ancient Egypt_. Baltimore.

Snijder, G.A.S.

    1936   _Kretische Kunst_. Berlin.

Vandier d'Abbadie, J.

    1937   _Catalogue des ostraca figurés de Deir el-Médineh_.
            Cairo.

Veenhof, K.R.

    1972   _Aspects of Old Assyrian Trade and its Terminology_.
            Leiden.

Vermeule, E.

    1975   _The Art of the Shaft Graves_. Cincinnati.

Ward, W.A.

    1972   A Unique Beset Figurine. _Orientalia_ 41: 149 - 59.

Warren, P.

    1969   _Minoan Stone Vases_. Cambridge.

Weingarten, J.

    1981   _The Zakro Master and His Place in Prehistory_.
            M. Litt. dissertation. Oxford.

Weybrouck, M.

    1939   Les Multiples formes du dieu Bès. _BMusArt_ 11:
            79 - 82.

Willetts, R.F.

    1955   _Aristocratic Society in Ancient Crete_. London.

Wilkinson, A.

    1971   _Ancient Egyptian Jewellery_. London.

Wilson, V.

    1975   The Iconography of Bes with Particular Reference to

the Cypriot Evidence. <u>Levant</u> 7: 77 - 103.

Xénaki-Sakellariou, A.

    1958a   <u>Les Cachets minoens de la Collection Giamalakis</u>
                (Ét. Crét. x). Paris.

    1958b   Sur le cachet prismatique minoen. In <u>Minoica</u>:
                <u>Festschrift Sundwall</u> (ed. E. Grumach) 451 -60.
                Berlin.

Younger, J.

    1973   <u>Towards the Chronology of Aegean Glyptic in the</u>
            <u>Late Bronze Age</u>. Doctoral dissertation. Cincinnati.

    1978   The Mycenae-Vapheio Lion Group. <u>AJA</u> 82: 285 - 99.

    1979   Origins of the Mycenae-Vapheio Lion Master. <u>BICS</u>
            26: 119 - 20.

Yoyette, J.

    1971   <u>Treasures of the Pharaohs</u>. Geneva.

Yule, P.

    1977   Technical Observations on Early Neopalatial Seal-
            impressions. <u>Kadmos</u> 16: 56 - 69.

    1980   <u>Early Cretan Seals</u>: <u>A Study of Chronology</u> (Marburger
            Studien zur Vor- und Frühgeschichte 4). Mainz.

PLATES

PLATE 6

THREE-SIDED PRISMS (LBA) OF SPHERICAL/ELLIPTICAL SHAPE

blank   blank

A. Onyx from Mycenae, Chamber tomb 518 (CMS i 153)

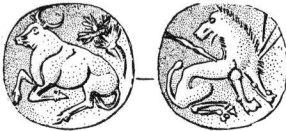

blank

B. From Ay. Ioannis, Warrior Grave III (BSA 47: 16,22)

C. Giam 187 "pierre dure ordinaire"

D. Giam 190 Chalcedony from Vasilika Anogeia

blank

E. Giam 186 Jasper from Mallia

blank

F. Carnelian from Kalyvia (MonAnt 14: 10 b,c)

PLATE 2

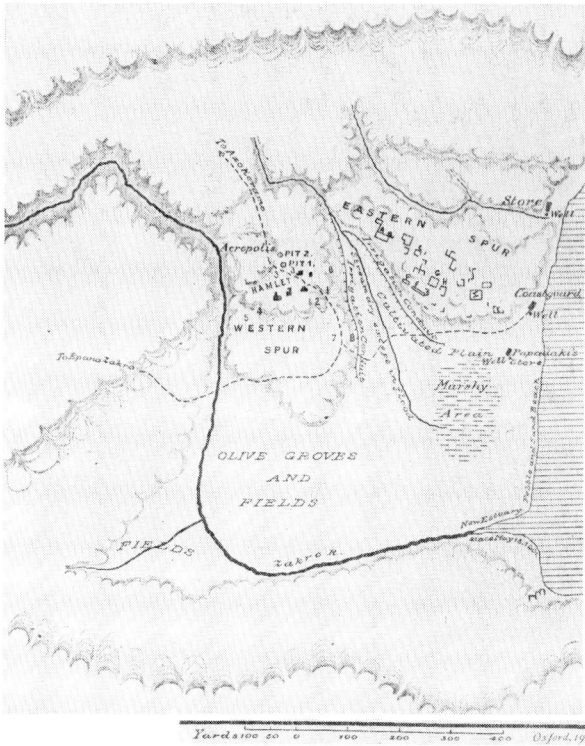

A. Sketch Map of the Zakro Delta (Hogarth 1901: 125; fig. A)

Fig. 43.—Typical Painted Vases from House A (1 : 5).

B. Hogarth 1901: fig. 43

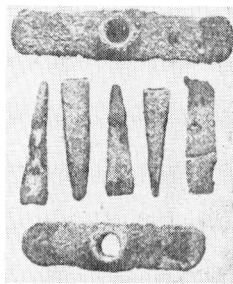

Fig. 44.—Bronze Knife, Mattocks and Drills from House A (1 : 4).

C. Hogarth 1901: fig. 44

PLATE 3

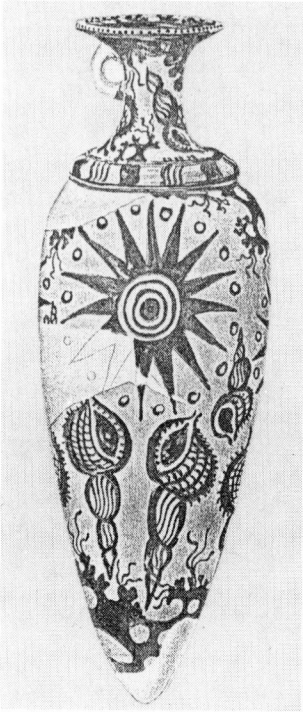

B. Marine rhyton from Zakro
Palace (Praktika 1962:
Pl. 153B)

A. Marine rhyton from Zakro
House A (Hogarth 1902a:
Pl. XII, 1)

FIG. 24.

FIG. 22.

FIG. 32.

FIG. 23.

C. More pottery from House A (Dawkins 1903: fig. 22, 23, 32)

PLATE 4

THREE-SIDED PRISMS (LBA) OF SPHERICAL/ELLIPTICAL SHAPE

A. Red jasper from Peloponnese? (CMS vii 115)

B. Red carnelian from Thebes (CMS v 677)

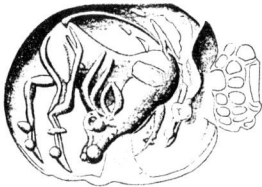

blank

C. Lapis lazuli with gold setting from Delos (CMS v 313)

D. Brown/cream carnelian (CMS v 191)

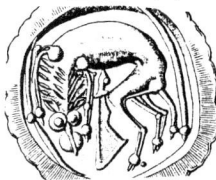

blank

E. Jasper from Pylos, Grave gamma (CMS i 287)

PLATE 5

THREE-SIDED PRISMS (LBA) OF SPHERICAL/ELLIPTICAL SHAPE

blank

A. Amethyst from Pylos Rutsi (CMS i 272)

blank

B. Amethyst from Pylos Rutsi (CMS i 273)

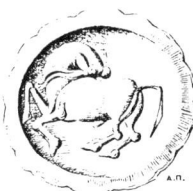

blank

C. Amethyst from Vapheio (CMS i 233)

blank

D. Agate from Midea, Chamber Tomb 10 (CMS i 193)

PLATE 1

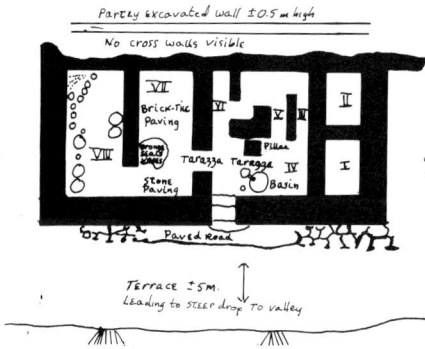

A. HOUSE A
   HOGARTH 1901: 131
   (slightly modified)

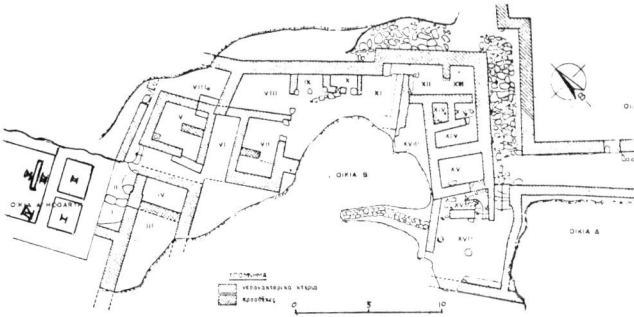

B. RECENT EXCAVATIONS ON
   EASTERN SPUR, ZAKRO
   PLATON 1979: Pl. 91
   (relationship to House A added)

PLATE 7

<u>LENTOIDS ENGRAVED ON BOTH FACES</u>

A.

B.

C.

D.

D.

E.

G.

 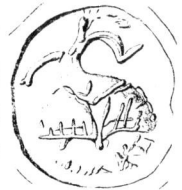

H.

I. (was Pl. 8 A)

J.

PLATE 8

LENTOIDS ENGRAVED ON BOTH FACES

B.

C. Published with the kind permission of the Scuola
    Archeologica Italiana di Atene

D.

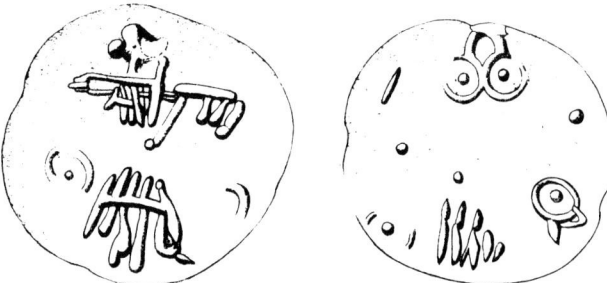

E.

PLATE 9

A.

B.

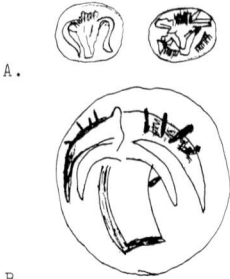

Bucrania on 3-sided
Steatite prisms
Ashmolean Museum
CS K 9, 10, 11

C.   D.
Mallia Stoneworking Atelier
Steatite 3-sided prisms
CMS ii/2 114a   CMS ii/2 120b

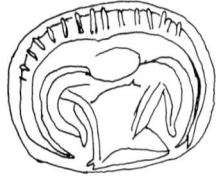

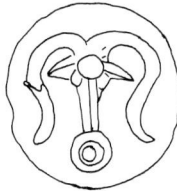

F.

Knossos sealing
Hieroglyphic Dep.
Matz, Frühkretischen
Siegel, Pl. 16, 11

E.
Zakro chance find
Rock crystal disk
CMS 11/2 283

G.
Green jasper/marble
Petschaft
CMS vii 34

H.
Knossos sealing
Room of the Stone
Bench: LM IIIA:1
Gill 1965: R 101

I.
Korakou
Steatite lentoid
CMS v 513

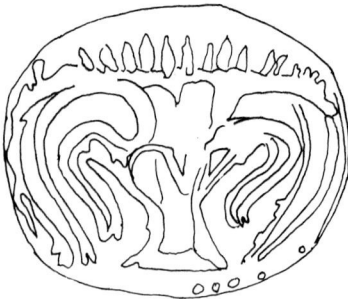

J.
3-sided
prism
HM 2208

K.
Sard/chalcedony
3-sided prism
CMS xii 162a

Plate 10

A. Knossos, carnelian
   4-sided prism
   PM i fig. 207 c-a

B,C
Mallia, chalcedony 4-sided prisms
Giam 112a, 109b

F. Knossos, stamp seal
   Giam 183

D,E
Mallia, steatite
3-sided prisms
Chapouthier 1946:
fig. 3
Chapouthier 1932:
185/2b

H. Mochlos, chalcedony
   Petschaft (CMS ii/2
   251)

G. Melos, painted pottery
   PM i 527c

K. Knossos, LMIB
   cup rhyton
   AR 27: 84 fig.34

I. Nichoria
   red carnelian
   lentoid
   (CMS v 431)

J. Melos, black & red
   painted pottery
   Hutchinson & Eccles 1940:
   Pl. 19,8

Plate 11

A. Steatite
3-sided prism
CMS ix 14a

B. Steatite
3-sided prism
CMS ix 3a

C. Steatite
3-sided prism
CMS viii 111c

D. Steatite
conoid
CMS viii 14

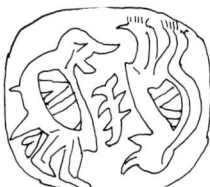

E. Mochos
Steatite
3-sided prism
CMS ii/2 219a

F. Phigalia?
rock crystal
lentoid
AGDS Berlin
54477

G. Mallia
Banded agate
hemicylinder
CMS iv 161

H. Phaestos
Painted pottery
Levi 1976:
Tab. lxvii b

I. Proph.Ilias,
Knossos
Silver disk
CMS ii/2 43

Plate 12

A.
Knossos HM 1411

B.
Phaestos sealing
CMS ii/5 323

C.
Phaestos sealing
CMS ii/5 214

D. Phaestos
Painted pottery
(detail)
Levi 1976:
Tab. lxv

E. Phaestos painted pottery
(detail)
Levi 1976: Tab. lxvii

F. Mallia
Steatite 3-sided prism
CMS ii/2 243a

G. Zakro House C?
Steatite 3-sided
prism (CMS ii/2
264a)

H. Mallia Palace
Quartier XIII
Steatite lentoid
Chapouthier &
Demargne 1942:
fig. 46a

Plate 13

A. Mallia Stoneworking Atelier
   Steatite cone (CMS ii/2 127)

B. Mallia, painted pottery
   Demargne 1932: fig. 1

C. Stone reel engraved on two faces
   Boardman 1970: fig. 80

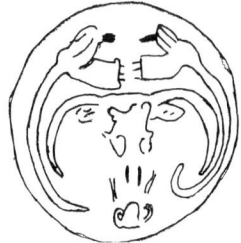

D. Psychro Cave (?)
   Haematite lentoid
   CS K 292

E. Knossos HM 137
   Smoky quartz
   amygdaloid

F. Steatite lentoid
   CS K 291

G. Haematite lentoid
   CS K 243a

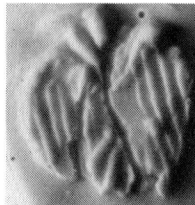

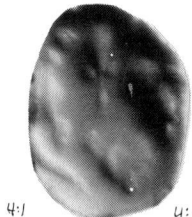

4:1

4:1

H. Ayia Triada sealings AT 100 + 101 found together
   on a single clay nodule (Class II)

I. AT 8

Plate 14

A. Sklavokampo sealings SK 13, 14, 16 found together, with
   SK 15, on a single clay "truncated polyhedron" (Marinatos
   1948: 90 - 91; Pl. iv 13, 14, 16)

B. Sklavokampo sealing SK 17
   Marinatos 1948: Pl. iv 17

C. Ayia Triada sealing AT 102

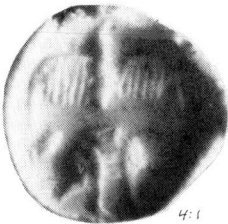

D. Ayia Triada sealing AT 103

E. Ayia Triada sealing
   AT 104 (Levi 1929a:
   fig. 120)

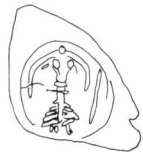

F. Ayia Triada
   sealing AT 105
   Levi 1929a:
   fig. 121

G. Palaikastro, cylinder seal
   BSA xl: 47, nr 26

Plate 15

A. Syro-Hittite cylinder seal
   2nd Syrian Group
   Contenau 1922: 176

B. Old Syrian cylinder seal
   Buchanan 1966: 899

C. Kerkouk, ca. 1500 B.C.
   Contenau 1926: 86

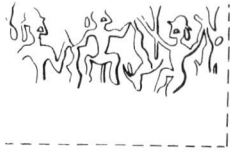

D. Mitannian, 15th c. B.C.
   Kantor 1962: fig. 10c

E. Mitannian, 15th c. B.C.
   Kantor 1962: fig. 10d

F. Kato Syme
   Agate lentoid
   Ergon 1976: fig. 158

G. Knossos sealing
   Queen's Megaron
   Gill 1965: R 103

H. Knossos (?)
   Basalt lentoid
   CMS xiii 84

I. Cyprus
   Haematite lentoid
   CMS vii 126

J. Pylos Palace
   sealing
   CMS i 324

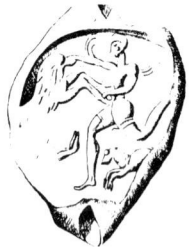

K. Mycenae sealing
   House, lower town
   CMS i 165

Plate 16

NEW KINGDOM IMAGES OF BES

A. XVIII Dynasty tomb wall relief (Säve-Söderbergh 1957: Pl. 35b)

B. Wood statuette
Louvre (Decamps de
Mertzenfeld 1938:fig.2)

C. Terracotta, Kahun
XIX Dynasty
Petrie 1890:8,14

D. Megiddo ivory plaque
13th century BC
Decamps de Mertzen-
feld 1938: 37,2

E. Ramesside wall painting
Smith 1965: fig. 57a

Plate 17

NEW KINGDOM IMAGES OF BES

A. Gilt stucco panels from XVIII Dynasty bed (Amenophis III)
(Davis, Maspero & Newberry 1907: Plate opposite p. 37)

B. Panel of chair of Sat-Amen
daughter of Amenophis III
(Davis, Maspero & Newberry
1907: 40; fig. 3)

C. Limestone head-rest
Deir el-Medina (XIX Dyn)
BM EA 63783; Photograph
courtesy of British Museum

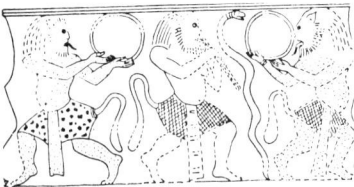

D. Painted jar, XVIII Dynasty
Smith 1965: fig. 57b

E. Gurob, pilgrim flask
- with LHIIIB stirrup jar
Petrie 1891: Pl. 17

Plate 18

NEW KINGDOM IMAGES OF BES
_____

2.8:1

B.
Faience amulet XVIII Dynasty
UC 30363; photograph courtesy
of Petrie Museum, University
College, London

A. Limestone ostrakon
   XIX Dynasty (?)
   EGA 4299 - 1943
   photograph courtesy of
   Fitzwilliam Museum
   Cambridge

D. Amulet worn by slave
   girl (outline draw-
   ing of ebony statue)
   Yoyotte 1968: Pl.95

E. Gurob Tomb 474 with
   LH IIIB stirrup jar;
   ivory amulet
   Brunton & Engleback
   1927: Pl. xxviii

C. limestone ostrakon
   Vandier d'Abbadie 1937:
   2622

F. Double signet ring
   Bes in two cartouches
   Wilkinson 1971:
   fig. 58

Plate 19

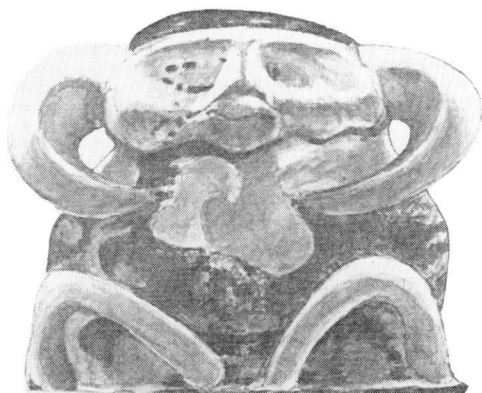

B. Phaestos (Levi 1976:Tab.lxixd)

A. Phaestos (Levi 1976:
   Tab. lxixb) NB: 6 fingers

D. Mallia (Detournay 1980:fig.168)

C. Unguent jar with Bes tattoo
   on wrists (Mogensen 1930:A540)

E. Dendereh, XI Dynasty clay vessel
   Ashmolean Museum E 1966

Plate 20

Z 20

Z 23

Z 37

Z 24(a)

Z 24(b)

Z 43

Z 25

Z 21

Z 26

Z 33

Z 173

Z 27

Plate 21

Z 129

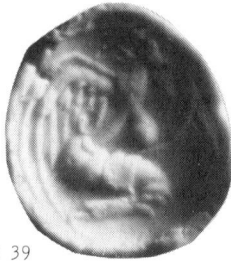

Z 39

Z 79

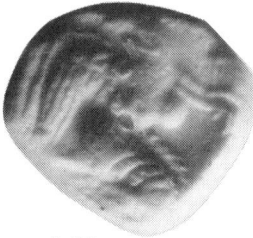

Z 38

Z 28

Z 29(a,b)

Z 34(a)

Z 34(b)

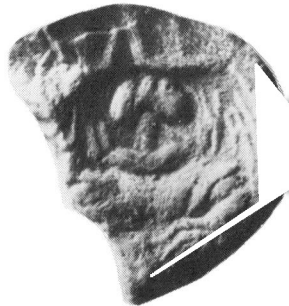

Z 32

Z 36(a)

Z 36(b)

Z 35

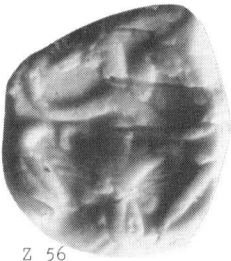

Z 56

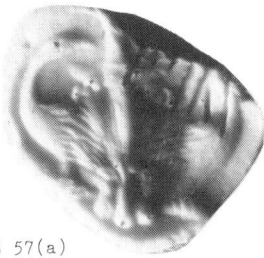

Z 57(a)

Plate 22

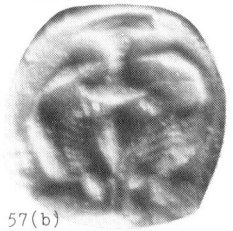

Z 57(b)

Z 60

Z 58(a)

Z 58(b)

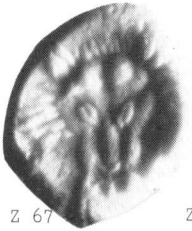

Z 67

Z Z 68

Z 69

Z 62

Z 66

Z 61(a)

Z 61(b)

Z 63

Z 64

Z 65

Z 59

Plate 23

Z 81

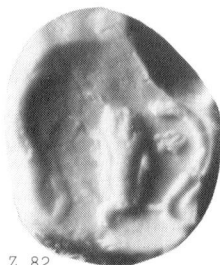

Z 82

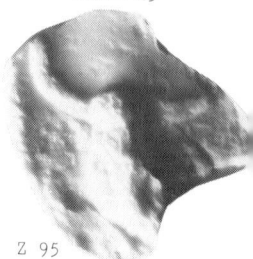

Z 95

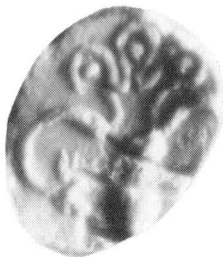

Z 83(a)

Z 83(b)

Z 165

Z 86

Z 87

Z 170

Z 17

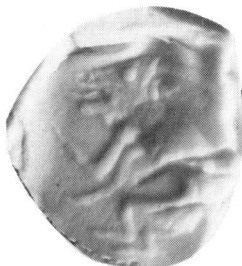

Z 18

Z 50

Plate 24

Z 52

Z 53

Z 54

Z 80

Z 51

Z 49

Z 89

Z 90

Z 48

Z 74

Z 71

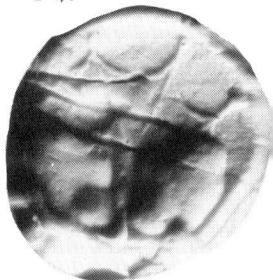

Z 77

Plate 25

Z 76

Z 75

Z 72

Z 78

Z 44

Z 45

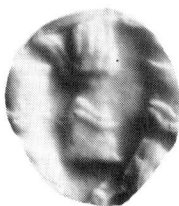

Z 46

Z 47

Z 22

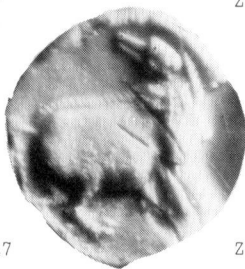

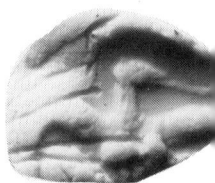

Z 70

Z 127

Z 55

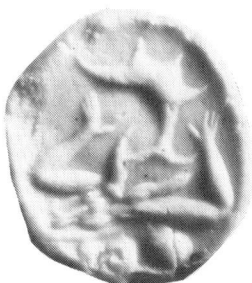

Z 92

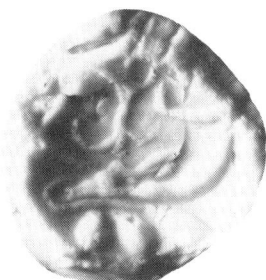

Z 92A

Z 139

Z 30

Z 73

Z 88

Z 31

Z 108

Z 111

Z 40

Z 42

Z 41

Plate 26

Z 128

Z 112(a)   Z 112(b)

Z 130

A. HM 1970
Royal Road, Knossos

B.
HM 614 Ax

C. <u>CMS</u> xii 255

D. <u>CMS</u> iv 290

E. <u>CMS</u> vii 143

F. HM 145
Ivory
Palaikastro

PLATE 27

1

2

3

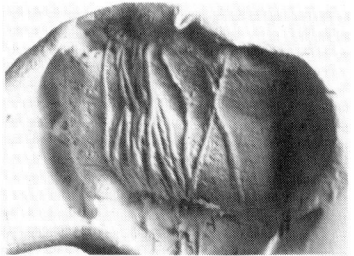

4

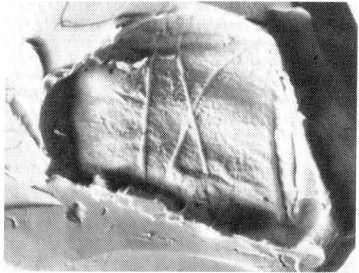

5

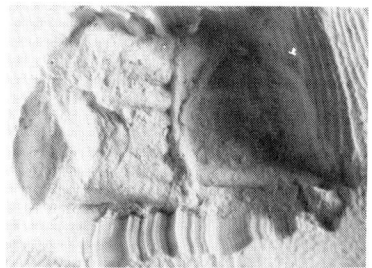

6

PLATE 28

7

8

9

10

11

12

PLATE 29

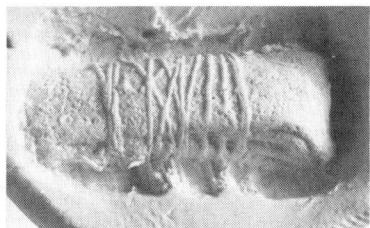

13

14

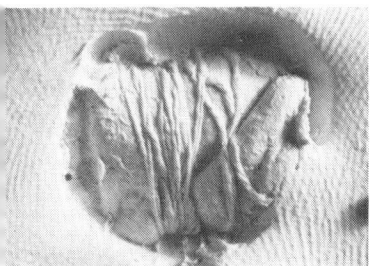

15

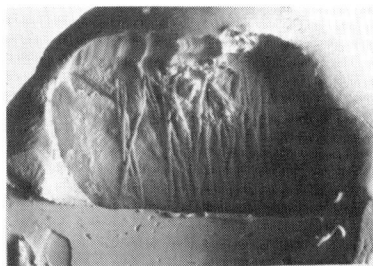

16

17

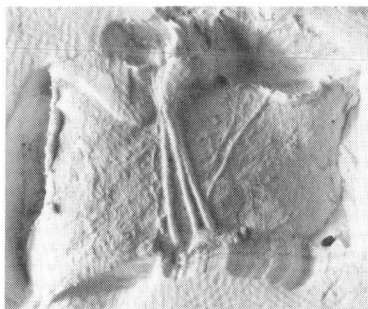

18

Invariable Combinations

MSS Nr 1   Nr 10 + 97

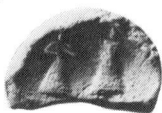

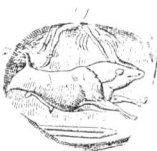

Z 10

Z 97
(Levi 1929b:fig.173)

MSS Nr 2   Nr 106 + 186/7

Z 106
(Levi 1929b:
fig. 176)

Z 186/7
(Levi 1929b:fig.225)

MSS Nr 3   Nr 104 + 119

Z 104

Z 119
HM 95

cf.: Nr 119 in the SSS
HM 64

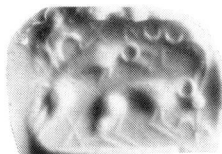

4:1

MSS Nr 4   Nr 193 + 227

Z 227

Z 193
(Levi 1929b:fig.
231)

Taurokathapsia
No illustration
available

MSS 5   Nr 3 + 102

Z 3   Z 102
                   (Levi 1929b:fig.174)

MSS 6   Nr 154 + 190

Z 154 (Levi 1929b: Z 190
       fig.192)   (Levi 1929b:fig.228)

MSS 7   Nr 155 + 237

Z 155   Z 237

MSS 8   Nr 192 + 238

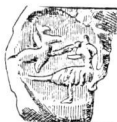   

Z 192 (Levi 1929b: Z 238
       fig. 230)

MSS 9   Nr 164 + 170

 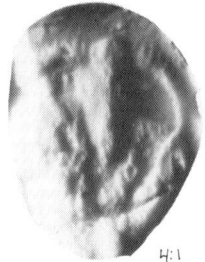

Z 164   Z 170

MSS 10   Nr 142 + 46

Z 142   Z 46

MSS 11   Nr 98 + 20 + 86

Z 98   Z 20   Z 86

MSS 12   Nr 196 + 72 + ??

    ??

Z 196 (Levi   Z 72
1929b:fig.234)

MSS Nr 13   Nr 71 + 89

Z 71   4:(Z 89   4:1

MSS 14   Nr 57 + 73

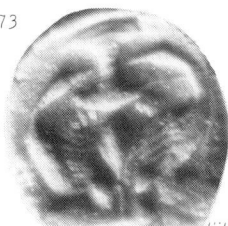 

Z 57   4:1   Z 73   3:1

MSS 15   Nr 36 + 64

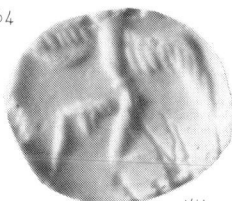 

Z 36   4:1   Z 64   4:1

MSS 16   Nr 80 + 134

Z 80   4:1   Z 134   3:1

MSS 17 Nr 23 + 52

Z 23   4:1   Z 52   4:1

MSS 18 Nr 17 + 127

Z 17   4:1   Z 127   4:1

MSS 19 Nr 39 + 43

Z 39   4:1   Z 43   4:1

MSS 20 Nr 18 + 83

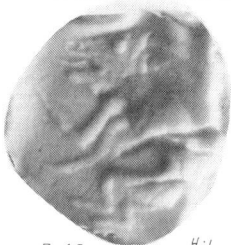 

Z 18   4:1   Z 83   4:1

MSS 21   Nr 34 + 236

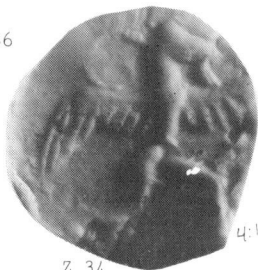

Z 34   Z 236

MSS 22   Nr 70 + 77

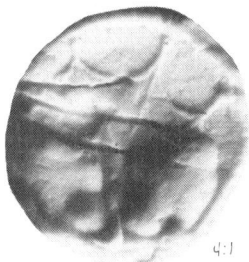

Z 70   Z 77

MSS 23   Nr 49 + 130

Z 49   Z 130

MSS 24   Nr 32 + 35

Z 32   Z 35

MSS 25   Nr 27 + 76

Z 27   Z 76

MSS 26   Nr 40 + 50

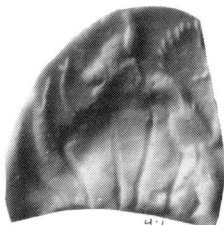

Z 40   Z 50

MSS 27   Nr 55 + 141

Z 55   Z 141

MSS 28   Nr 44 + 48 + 78

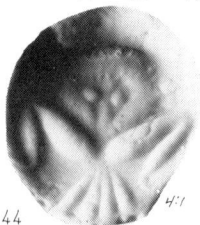

Z 44   Z 48   Z 78

MSS 29 Nr 25 + 45 + 53

Z 25   Z 45   Z 53

MSS 30 Nr 58 + 84 + 74

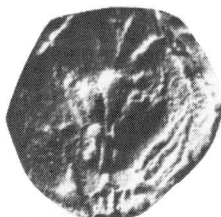  

Z 58   Z 84   Z 74

MSS 31 Nr 81 + 82 + 108

 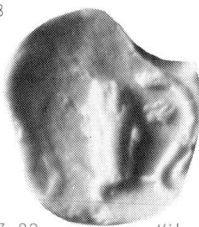 

Z 81   Z 82   Z108

MSS 32 Nr 79 + 93 + 111

Z 79   Z 93   Z 111

MSS 33   Nr 38 + 167 + 68

Z 38   Z 167   Z 68

<u>Variable Combinations</u>

MSS 34   Nr 2 + 62
MSS 35   Nr 2 + 26
MSS 36   Nr   26 + 66

Z 2   Z 62

Z 2   Z 26

Z 26   Z 66

MSS 37   Nr 12/13 +   75
MSS 38   Nr 12/13 +   87
MSS 39   Nr 12/13 + 113
MSS 40   Nr 12/13 + 184
MSS 41   Nr 12/13 + 175

Z 12/13

Z 75

Z 12/13

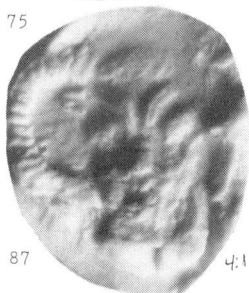

Z 87

Z 12/13

Z 113

Z 12/13

Z 184 (Levi 1929b:fig. 222)

Z 12/13

Z 175 (Levi 1929b:fig.213)

MSS 42   Nr 15 + 37 + 54
MSS 43   Nr 15 + 59 + 135
MSS 44   Nr 15 + 218

Z 15

Z 37

Z 54

Z 15

Z 59

Z 135

Z 15

Z 218

MSS 45   Nr 24 + 112 + 60
MSS 46   Nr 24 + 112 + 105

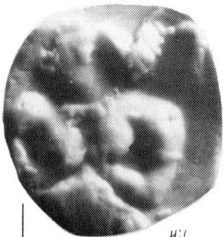

Z 24

Z 112

Z 60

Z 24   Z 112   Z 105 (Betts 1967:fig.8a)

MSS 47   Nr 51 + 131 + 19
MSS 48   Nr 51 + 131 + 85

Z 51   3:1   Z 131   3:1   Z 19

Z 51   Z 131   Z 85

MSS 49   Nr 21 + 61 + 28
MSS 50   Nr 21 + 61 + 29
MSS 49A/
    50A   Nr 21 + 61A + 28/29?

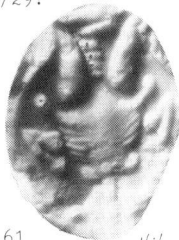

Z 21   4:1   Z 61   4:1   Z 28   3:1

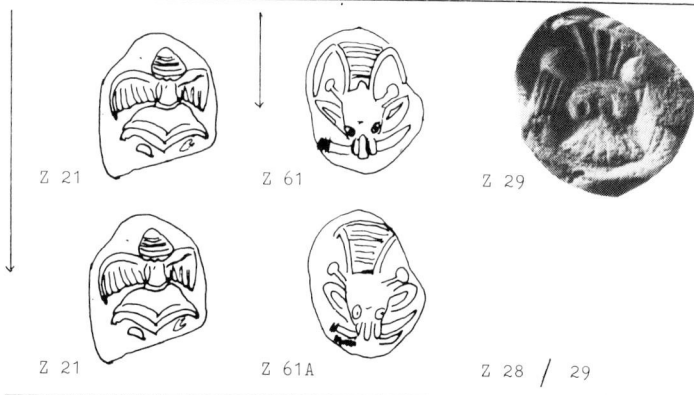

Z 21   Z 61   Z 29

Z 21   Z 61A   Z 28 / 29

MSS 51   Nr 22 + 63
MSS 52   Nr 22 +   + 56
MSS 53   Nr   63 + 56

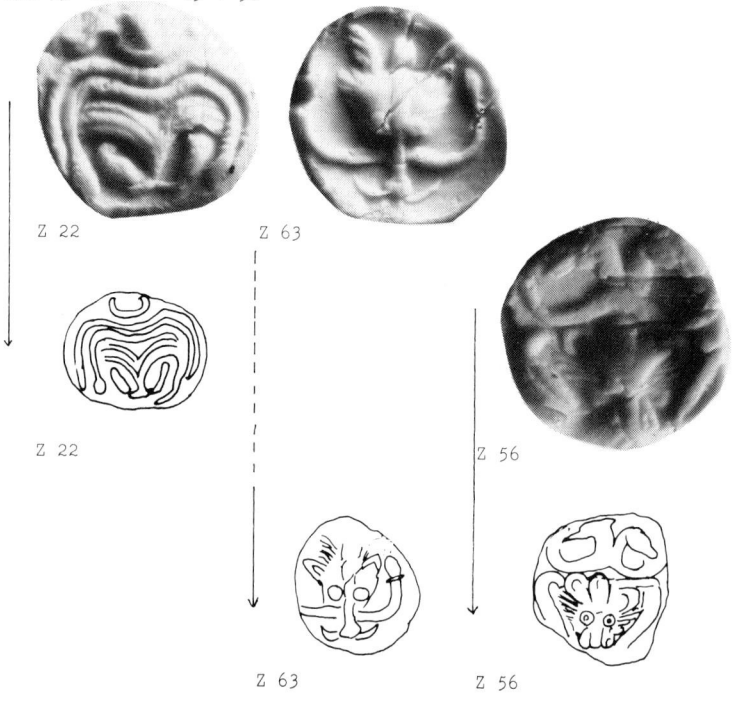

Z 22   Z 63

Z 22   Z 56

Z 63   Z 56

MSS 54   Nr 69 +   67 + 30
MSS 55   Nr 69 + 171 + ??

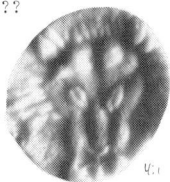

Z 69   Z 67   Z 30

Z 69   Z 171 (Levi 1929b: ??
                      fig. 209)

MSS 56   Nr 90 + 132 +   33
MSS 57   Nr 90 + 132 + 173
MSS 58   Nr 90 + 132 +   88

Z 90   Z 132   Z 33

Z 90   Z 132   Z 173

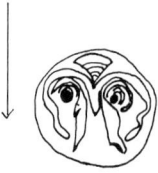 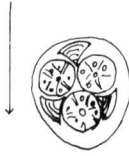 

Z 90   Z 132   Z 88   4:1

MSS 59   Nr 129 + 92
MSS 60   Nr 129 + 92A
MSS 61   Nr 129 + 139

 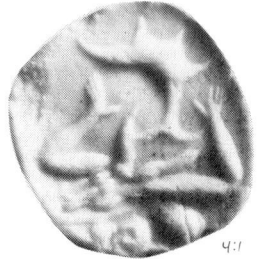

Z 129   4:1   Z 92   4:1

 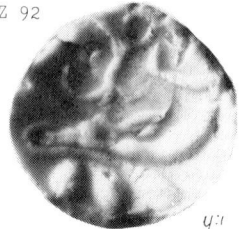

Z 129   Z 92A   4:1

 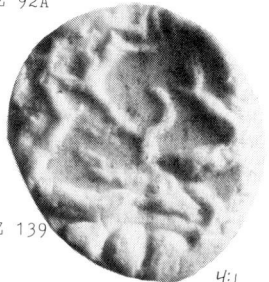

Z 129   Z 139   4:1

SEALINGS FROM ZAKRO.

SEALINGS FROM ZAKRO.

SEALINGS FROM ZAKRO.

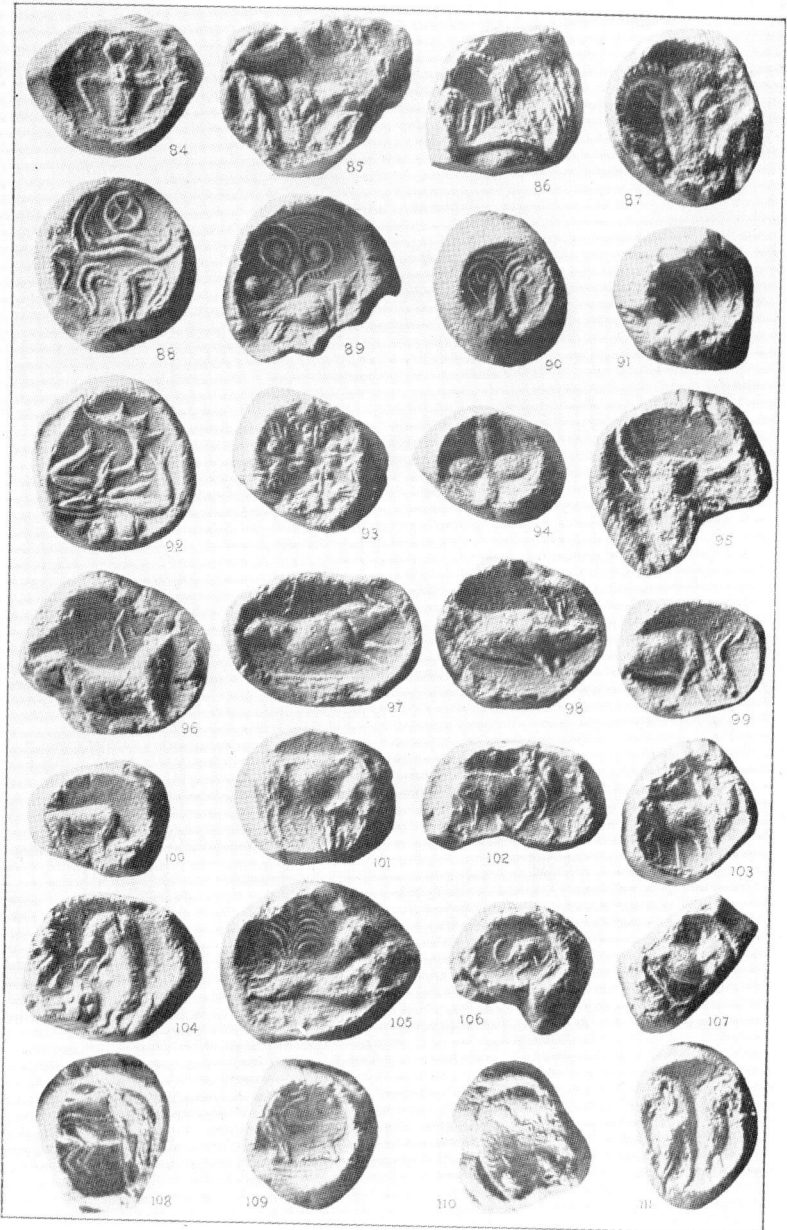

SEALINGS FROM ZAKRO.

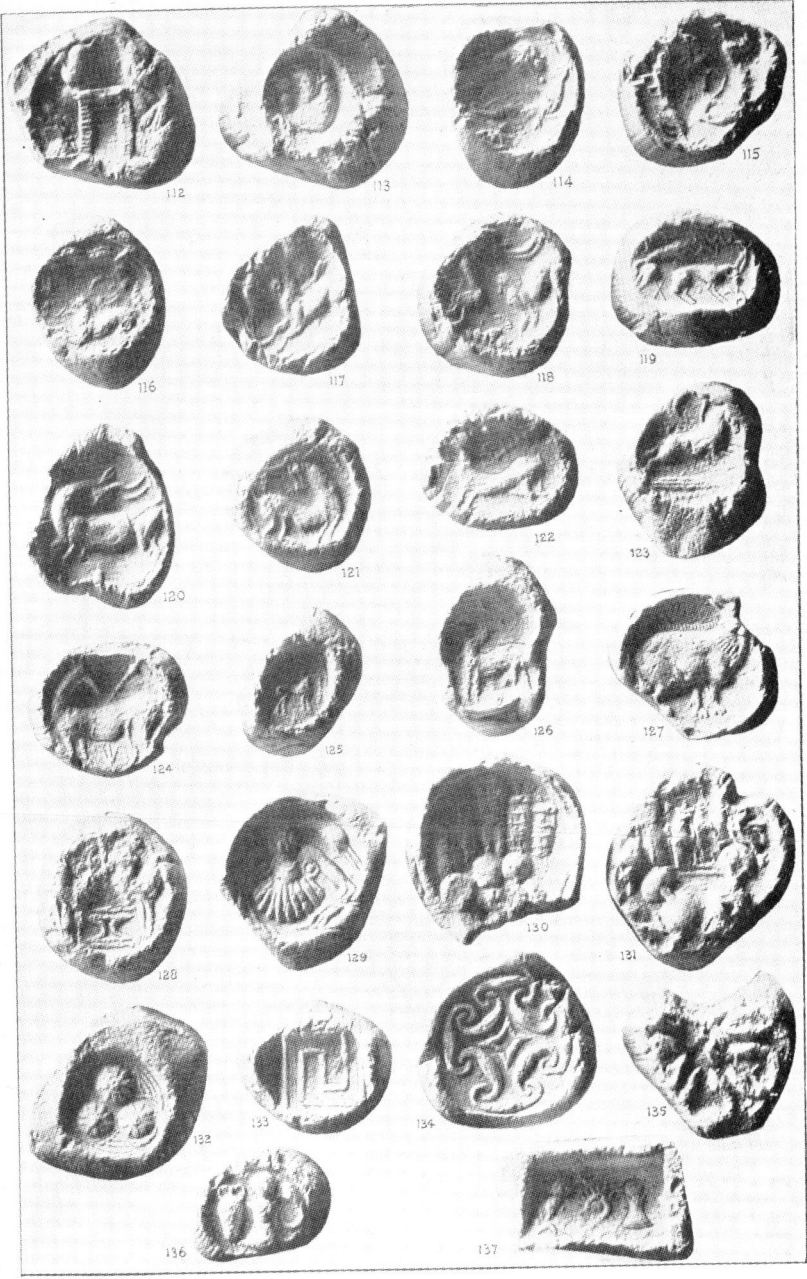

SEALINGS FROM ZAKRO.